MY YEARS WITH CORRIE

MY YEARS
WITH CORRIE

**ELLEN DE KROON
STAMPS**

KINGSWAY PUBLICATIONS
EASTBOURNE
and
CHRISTIAN LITERATURE CRUSADE
ALRESFORD

ISBN 0 86065 073 1

Unless otherwise indicated, Scripture quotations are from
the Authorized Version of the Bible.

Scripture quotations identified LB are from
The Living Bible, © Tyndale House Publishers 1971.
All rights reserved.

Scripture quotations identified PHILLIPS are from
The New Testament in Modern English (Revised Edition)
translated by J. B. Phillips, © J. B. Phillips 1958, 1960, 1972.

Printed in Great Britain for
KINGSWAY PUBLICATIONS LTD
*Lottbridge Drove, Eastbourne, E. Sussex BN23 6NT by
Hunt Barnard Printing Ltd., Aylesbury, Bucks.*

Contents

Ellen and I

Together on the front line of the work for the Kingdom of God. We both knew that it was not our strength, our victory, when we experienced blessings from the Lord. We both knew for ourselves:

> He never gives in
> And we two will win,
> Jesus and I.

This book tells of our going together as tramps for the Lord – and Jesus was Victor. That is why His victory was demonstrated.

Jesus, Ellen, and I.

CORRIE TEN BOOM

Introduction

The airport was bustling with summer travellers – business-men and holiday-makers arriving and departing with the excitement of happy reunions and the anticipation of new adventures. I was excited too, yet with a different excitement than I had once felt. Long ago I lost count of the times I had stepped off planes – to be greeted by Christian friends with outstretched arms of love in distant parts of the world and many cities in the United States. This time I was on the *waiting* end. With me was my dear husband, Bob, and in my arms, our precious two-month-old son, Peter John, who didn't quite understand the bouquet of tulips and narcissi in his lap.

Soon our guest arrived, and what a joy it was to transfer my bundle of baby and flowers into her open arms. As always seemed to happen, others in the airport recognized her. I instinctively moved to shield her from the attention of the crowds. Then I realized this wasn't my responsibility any more – someone else was at her side to take care of her – and I moved back just as one woman exclaimed, 'Oh, is that your grandchild?'

Our guest looked up at her with her big blue eyes and said, 'Oh, yes, and a very special one.' Then she glanced at me with that twinkle in her eyes that I had come to know so well. Little Peter John was to her the grandchild no daughter would ever be able to give her. And as for Peter John, this was his first meeting with his grandmother Johanna – or to us, Corrie ten Boom. (Corrie has three names: Cornelia, Arnolda, and Johanna. We chose the last, to make her even more special.)

Corrie had come for Peter John's dedication and baptismal service. My mother had come to Tulsa from Holland. Bob's

9

parents had driven up from Texas. My dear friends, Mike and Fran Ewing, Peter John's godparents, were present from Florida. In the service, Corrie shared a text from Hebrews: 'May he effect in us everything that pleases him through Jesus Christ, to whom be glory forever and ever. Amen' (Hebrews 13:21 PHILLIPS). Corrie later wrote: 'We human beings look at little babies with so much love and appreciation and joy, but we sometimes forget that the most important thing is how *God* sees His children. I read in Zephaniah 3:17: " . . . Is that a joyous choir I hear? No, it is the Lord himself exulting *over you* in happy song" ' (LB, italics added).

Peter John had brought great joy into our lives, but what a greater privilege to know that God rejoices over the life of *each* of His children, young and old alike. He carefully plans our lives and gives us such excitement when we trust in Him. Just as Corrie had called Peter John *special*, so the Lord calls each of His children special. I was very aware of this that summer in Tulsa – aware anew of how He had taken care of me and brought about so many changes in my life. A few years ago, I could never have imagined waiting to greet Corrie ten Boom in an airport in the middle of Oklahoma. In fact, I could not have imagined even knowing Corrie ten Boom or ever visiting Oklahoma!

This is a book, then, about God's great imagination – about how He can and does order our lives to prepare us for His wonderful gifts, which are beyond our greatest dreams. To a great extent, it is Corrie's story too. For nine years, I had been in her presence constantly as her travelling companion. As my husband says, I was tramping with the Tramp for the Lord around the world. It is a story about how God can use us, even when we feel unusable, how He loves us, even when we feel unlovable, and how He rejoices over His children – and that means you and me!

I

The Winter of 1944

The months of Nazi occupation in Holland had lengthened into years. Holland gradually became a nation of old people, women, and children. All our men, except those needed to maintain the necessities of our society and those who went into hiding, were systematically deported to Germany to work its factories. One of these men was my father.

My own arrival into this world was quite different from our son's thirty-seven years later. My family was living in a little village, suburb of Rotterdam in the Netherlands. We had a small house in a row of four, with a little lawn in the front and a larger one in the back. I was born in that house on June 8, 1940, and welcomed by my father, mother, two brothers, and a sister. I am told it was a beautiful day with nice white clouds drifting across the sky. But the beauty of the day was marred by the sounds of war.

Just one month before I was born, Hitler's armed forces had invaded our country. Our own city had been bombed mercilessly and our Dutch army had surrendered in a matter of days. I arrived in a world of terrible tension, fear, hunger, and unbelievable suffering. My mother tells me I was a very heavy baby and the hardest for her to bring into the world. I have often thought about that – maybe the Lord was giving me a good start because He alone knew what was ahead in the next five years when growling stomachs and hungry mouths were to become common and the weak often died.

Because it was a nice day, warm and sunny, Mother had the midwife put me into our wooden cradle and roll it outside in the garden. I started my life in fresh air with green grass and garden flowers. Maybe that is one of the reasons I still love the outdoors so much. The sun is still a good friend of mine – you should see how it changes my face into a mass of freckles which make me look even more like the Dutch girl that I am!

That first trip into life and out into the garden was to be followed by many other trips in my lifetime – some of them to faraway lands and unusual situations. But none of them was quite the same as the journey I was to take when I was four, when the brown wooden wheels of the cradle were to be replaced by the wheels of a little red wagon.

Life became especially hard for my mother and us children during the cold winter months. I remember breathing on the frozen windowpanes to make a little hole so we could see outside. In those days, there was not much to see on our little street. No petrol means no cars. All we could see was the white countryside and flurries of snow as the wind picked up the loose flakes and blew them about. Many people in Holland must have felt as helpless as the snowflakes being whipped about with an uncertain destiny.

In the winter of 1944, my mother became deeply troubled. She had five children. I was four, and my younger sister was only a year old. I had two older brothers and an older sister. What was a mother to do, with five near-starving little ones and her husband in a German work camp? What to eat and wear? How to keep warm and survive the winter?

The school just around the corner from us had been taken over by the Germans as their headquarters in our area; it was also the distribution kitchen for food – such as it was. The food became so bad that mothers resorted to feeding the families tulip bulbs, and when there was no food, sleep became an antidote to hunger. When we slept, we forgot our stomachs. We would all six sleep huddled together in my parents' big bed, so that the warmth of our bodies would make up for the lack of heat in our house. The only other warm place in the house was the kitchen, but only if my oldest brother and mother could find firewood in their secret journeys after dark. More and more throughout our little village, the fires went out in the stoves and no smoke curled up from the chimneys.

One day our neighbour called my mother over to her house and showed her a beautiful blue woollen coat. 'I already have a coat, and I want to give this one to you.' Mother took the coat and made a little coat and hat for me that same night. Mother later told me, 'God gave you a warm, beautiful little blue outfit for a long and difficult trip.' There was no earthly father at home to take care of us, but the heavenly Father provided.

Later that winter Mother received word from our pastor that some farmers in eastern Holland could help feed and take care of us children. With that good news came some bad news – not all of us could go. Two must stay behind. It was a difficult decision for my mother. How she must have wrestled with her thoughts. But finally the decision was made – better to separate and live, than to stay together and starve. Many families across Holland were making the same agonizing decisions.

A rather good friend who lived near us offered to keep my two sisters; Ronnie, who was then eight years old, and Loes, the youngest at twelve months. Ronnie could be like a little mother to the baby. My mother had no other choice. All our family's food stamps would remain behind with them, which would insure food for my sisters and in part for the family who took them. The boys, Arthur and Frederick, were invited to stay on different farms where there were boys their age, and I was invited to stay with a family that had expressed a desire to have a little girl. God must have given my mother extra grace the day when she had to leave her two daughters behind, not knowing what the future would hold and if she would ever see them again.

Mother put me into our little red wagon, which represented happy occasions to me: a trip to the playground *Plaswyck*, the swimming pool, *Het Zwarte Plasje*, or a walk. We set off late one afternoon on our journey. Before we reached the main road, where a truck was to pick us up, we had to pass Grandmother and Grandfather's house. Grandfather had his cobbler's shop in the back of their home. I can still vividly remember the years after the war, when we passed that house on our way to school. Grandma and Grandfather would act out the same scene every day: Grandma would wait by the window until all the grandchildren had passed by and then, but only then, she would make a cup of coffee for herself and Grandfather. Through all my school years, that was a stable point in my life. Now that I am an adult, I realize that Grandma's desire to see all her grandchildren pass by each day may have been a reaction to that day when she watched us walk away, not knowing where we were to go or what would become of us. Separation from loved ones is always difficult, but it is even harder when times are uncertain.

The lane ended at the road atop the dike that sheltered our little village. We knew the place well. On the right side was the playground. Now the pond by the zoo was frozen, and the red-cheeked, smiling boys and girls who should have been skating on the ice were missing. So were the vendors, with their hot chocolate and thick pea soup – and so was that good *polka-brokken* candy! We felt fortunate just to have some tins of Grandma's brown beans tucked away around me in our red wagon. That was our food security for the next few days.

We must have been a pitiful sight as our family and several others huddled together on the old truck bed. We looked back at the home village we were leaving behind – red tile roofs peeping out from heavy blankets of snow in the dusk, here and there smoke spiraling thinly upwards from the chimneys. It was a dismal scene. Still, I felt safe with Mother and my big brothers. After some hours we stopped. The driver of the truck had been told there was an old barn that could offer us some shelter for the night, but the barn was gone – a victim of the war.

The truck ended its mission and we began our long walk, first passing the city of Amersfoort, a silent procession, all of us peering straight ahead. In Voorthuizen, some miles further, Mother found a school where children were being fed, and we all ate well for the first time in months. But we must have eaten too much, because that night we children were in a terrible condition. We were staying in an upstairs room and the staircase was very steep; the toilet facilities were outside. Mother had to make that dreadful trip downstairs with us each time. The first time we went down, we were in for a shock – there was a mirror on the inside of the door, and we thought we had walked into a stranger. In the middle of the night, with hurting tummies, standing outside in the icy cold, afraid of our own images in the mirrors – everything seemed very dark in our lives.

During that time, Corrie had just returned from the concentration camp in Germany. She was already telling her story, including how lonely she had been at Ravensbruck. One night she had prayed in the camp, 'God. You have the stars under Your control. Have You forgotten me?' My mother must have thought the same thing that night.

My younger brother was especially sick, but Mother had no choice but to bundle us up the next morning and move on. We travelled on foot for days, begging food from families along the way, mother pulling me in the little red wagon.

At one farm we were given a head of a yellow cabbage. Later we were stopped by a German soldier, and he took a piece of that cabbage out of my brother Arthur's hands, thinking it was cheese. When he discovered it was only cabbage, he angrily threw it over a fence. Mother told me later that Arthur just stood there, his hands empty, bedazzled that someone could be so cruel and crazy enough to throw away food.

On one of the nights when the rain was coming down in seeming buckets, Mother made a shelter for us in a haystack. Like a mother hen, she made a little nest for us where we tried to keep warm and to sleep. When we were almost asleep we heard voices – German men were talking nearby. Mother whispered to us to lie very still and not make a sound. As I grew older and became a woman, I began to understand the danger Mother faced on our journey. That night must have been for her a very long night.

Ten days after we left our house in Rotterdam, we came to the end of our journey. We had not been out of our clothes, and we were unbelievably tired and hungry. I remember walking down a long lane with very high pine trees on either side. We saw no houses, no farms. That lane appeared as long as our entire walk had been, yet the hope of a real bed and food prodded us on. Soon, some houses and farms came into view. My younger brother, Frederick, stayed at the first farm. I stayed at the next. My mother went on with my older brother, Arthur, to stay at a farm about an hour away. She worked there, but made regular visits to see Frederick and me.

I could not understand the people I stayed with – they spoke a different dialect of Dutch than my family. One of their daughters bathed me and fed me right away. Years later, Mother told me that the people said I never uttered a word while staying with them. Nor did I cry. Actually, I didn't learn to talk well until after I was five years old. I was so frightened, I was speechless.

The farmhouse was small, rather dark, with few windows. The little room where I slept with other members of the family was slightly higher than the rest of the house. A plank with blocks of wood served as a staircase for the slight incline. That same plank served as the cellar door. Underneath my bed was the food supply for the entire house. I could smell the food, and yet now I wasn't hungry. What a different situation that was for me! I still remember the clean bed and the nice pillow in that room. The farmers were happy to have a little fair-haired girl, and they protected me as one of their own.

Occasionally word came to us that German soldiers were on their way. The farmer and his wife would quickly hide their most precious possessions and take their animals into the nearby woods for protection. We would flee to a special place in the woods – a dry ditch with lots of leaves. We would stay there until Uncle Jansen, the farmer, would tell us that all was safe and we could return home. On one of the trips back to the house I had my first encounter with death – the old faithful shepherd dog had been shot.

The historians now call that winter of 1945 in Holland 'The Hungry Winter'. But the worst of all the winters brought the best of the springs – Germany surrendered in May, and Father came home. My grandmother came to pick me up from the farm, and we returned to Rotterdam.

Our people dedicated themselves to rebuilding their country, but oh, the destruction – factories, railroads, our great harbours so crippled. And there was so much flooding as a result of damage to the dikes. It was a time for rebuilding out of devastation, and my school years were also to become a time of rebuilding for me – a time for God to take a shy, scared, speechless little Dutch girl and rebuild her life.

2

Rebuilding

Mother never allowed hatred to be harboured in our lives. I believe that is one of the greatest gifts a mother can give her children. I cannot remember hearing my mother say anything against the German people. When I travelled to Germany and other countries later in my life, it was good to be free of bitterness.

My father, who was an epileptic as a result of a fall in his childhood, came back from the German work camp emotionally broken and a sick man. We children learned quickly that it was no shame to help provide for ourselves and our brothers and sisters. Mother always knew how to 'bind the beginning to the end of the week,' as we Dutch say. She was very careful with her money and sewed everything for us. During the war, she made us new clothes from curtains and Father's cast-offs. She was resourceful and innovative in all she did. Many times I look back with thanks for the skills I learned from my mother.

Because of my slow start with speech and language, I found school difficult – especially reading and writing – and I had no hopes of going on to higher education. Foreign languages, a prerequisite for college, were especially difficult for me. Then, too, my family was not highly educated, so college was not expected for any of us. Still, school days were fun. We had two ways of going to school – one over the dike past Grandma's house and through the village, the other across the drainage ditches and through the cow pastures. In the winter we could always tell if the ice in the ditches was safe to cross, because the windmills would quit turning. From my desk I could see houses across the little pond in front of our school, and I would watch the mothers cleaning their homes and having their morning coffee. I often daydreamed about my mother at home, and I looked forward to one day having a family of my own.

After the six years of elementary school, I chose to go into home economics, a two-year course. Then when I was fifteen, I went to help in the house of a doctor's family. I had dreamed of being a nurse since I was a small child, and I hoped this experience would give me an insight into the world of medicine. I learned to take care of their baby and to clean house as well. Momma was very eager for her children to become acquainted with people who could teach us things that she could not. She was aware that she could not give us everything, so she was glad when I had the opportunity to become part of that good doctor's family.

I left the doctor's family to work in a chemist's shop in the centre of Rotterdam. I worked and studied there for two more years to become a pharmacist, but still with the final goal of becoming a nurse. In Holland, many of the professions are learned through apprenticeships, including nursing. Nursing study was usually a practical course taught within the hospitals. My training at the chemist's shop helped me to get ready for nurse's training and for work in the hospital. I spent the next three years there, working and studying simultaneously. What a great day it was when I finally graduated from nursing training. It was like a dream come true to have that S.R.N. pin proudly fastened on my spotless, starched white uniform.

During my second year at the hospital, I met several Christians. I had been a church member all my life, and my mother had taught me little songs about Jesus to sing when I was afraid. We always said the Lord's Prayer around our supper table. I had a knowledge of God, but He wasn't a personal reality to me. I had never read the Bible or prayed by myself.

These new Christian friends invited me to a retreat for

young people. Actually, it was a three-week Bible-study camp in Austria, and my friends who were going were also planning to help the people in the war refugee camps nearby. Most of them were people from communist countries. That appealed to my sense of social responsibility, so I decided to go along. I hadn't counted on seven o'clock Bible studies each morning! Never had I seen such prayer and praise! These people were different from the churchgoers I had known. At the end of the second week the group leader, Sidney Wilson, from Scotland, asked me to make tea for the group. I felt so inadequate, so un-qualified to do *anything* in the midst of this group that I said, 'No. Why don't you ask your Christians to do it?' He realized my need and took the time right then and there to explain privately to me how I could have Jesus in my life, and he actually helped me to make that step. Up until that time I knew how to know Jesus with my head, but I had never made any application of that knowledge to my heart and soul. Once, even before I made my own decision for the Lord, an elderly woman in the hospital had asked me how she could give her heart to Jesus. I had pulled out a tract someone had given me and read her what it said to do. She found peace with God through that, but I had never followed my own instructions! There in Austria I accepted Jesus as my Friend, my Saviour, and Lord of *my* life.

I came back to Holland and became involved with the Blum-hard Fellowship gatherings. Blumhard was a minister from Germany, who had a great and liberating Gospel message. At his meetings, people's lives were changed and God's power manifest. The theme of his ministry was a phrase he often quoted: *Jesus ist Sieger* or 'Jesus is Victor.' Corrie ten Boom first heard that phrase from the Blumhard people and she has since made it popular around the world. One Friday evening, Corrie and her secretary Conny came to speak at our fellow-ship gathering. I have never forgotten the message she gave that evening. She spoke about how we are a garden of the Lord. ' "We are no wilderness, but a garden of the Lord." Those were Spurgeon's words. We are walled around by grace, visited by love, weeded by heavenly discipline, planted by instruction, and guarded by divine power. One soul so favoured is prepared to yield fruit to the glory of God.'

I responded strongly to her message about being prepared to yield fruit to the glory of God – especially since I was planning to become a missionary myself – a missionary nurse.

After completing my nursing training, I realized that though my professional skills were very adequate, my evangelistic skills, if we may call them that, were not. Therefore, I joined the evangelical missionary society, Operation Mobilization, for a year, to learn methods of evangelism. Once again, Austria became the place of my spiritual pilgrimage. I returned to work in house-to-house literature distribution. I loved the ministry and the people, though still having it in my mind to one day be a missionary *nurse*. My heart now seemed to be leading me to continue working with Operation Mobilization, this time in the Middle East.

I had returned to Holland, to pack my bags for the Middle East, when a Christian friend in Driebergen asked me to come and spend two weeks helping her and her pregnant daughter. When these friends heard of my plans, they strongly discouraged my trip to Lebanon and advised instead that I return to Utrecht for more training at the university clinic. I had my plans all made for Lebanon, but after much time in prayer those two weeks, I could see the wisdom of their counsel. So I returned to Utrecht for more study in gynaecological/obstetrics. Someone once said, 'Big doors swing on little hinges.' That decision to remain in Holland and in nursing kept me in the centre of God's will and ready for the next big step. How *big*, I would not have dreamed!

In the evenings I worked with a group of young people who had opened a coffeehouse as part of a street ministry. I would go out with a friend or group, taking the Gospel wherever I could, sitting with young people on the streets and talking to them about Jesus. We ran the coffeehouse ourselves, and there was always something exciting happening for the Lord. I enjoyed this work with our young people so much, although

I still intended to be a missionary in a poor and needy foreign country.

One weekend I drove my motorbike back up to Driebergen for the morning service at our church. One of the members, Mrs Rie-Ypma, confronted me with a new challenge.

I didn't know it then, but she was a special friend of Corrie. I knew her as a faithful servant of the Lord, who had made many trips behind the Iron Curtain, her car loaded with 'bread' (Bibles) and clothing. She always seemed to have so much love to give away. Many times it seemed the Lord sent His angels to help her get into and out of those countries safely. Mrs Rie-Ypma came to me and said, 'Ellen, every time I pray for Corrie ten Boom, the Lord tells me to pray for you. Ellen, Corrie needs a new secretary, and the Lord is telling me you are the person. Why don't you go over to see her?'

I knew how much time Mrs Rie-Ypma spent praying, and when I heard her talk like that, I suddenly became scared. I said, 'Oh, no. That is impossible. I am a nurse, not a secretary. I work with young people, not old people. I can do many things, but imagine my working as a secretary with a woman who is seventy-five years old! Why don't you pray for someone else?'

She said simply, 'Ellen, maybe you can help her.' And she left it like that. The word *help* reached my heart. Yes, I might be able to help. But help, to me, meant giving her a cup of tea or visiting her now and then. Why should I be afraid to *help* a little? It certainly couldn't interfere with my life's goals. So I accepted an invitation to meet with Corrie ten Boom.

3

Meeting the Tramp

It was a beautiful Sunday in the summer of 1967 that I made
my way to visit Corrie for the first time. She was living in an
apartment in Soestdijk. After church I boarded the yellow bus
in Driebergen and set out on the hour-long ride. I tried to
picture the meeting with Corrie. I had seen her only once, at
that Blumhard Fellowship meeting. I remembered her grey-
white hair with the soft roll, her high forehead, and her gentle,
lined face. She wore heavy black shoes and dressed as other
Dutch women her age – very conservatively and very plainly.
I knew she was in her mid-seventies and that she and
Brother Andrew had recently returned from a trip through
Vietnam.

As the wheels of the bus brought me closer to Corrie's place,
I became more nervous. Ever since I had become a Christian
three years before, I knew that I wanted to serve the Lord, but
I still had much to learn about a walk of faith and trust.

I rang the bell of the block of flats. I glanced around – it was
a gorgeous summer day. Lovely flowers surrounded the
building. A main road and two driveways separated this building from the royal palace. I had heard that Corrie was living in
the apartment of a baroness. Frankly, I was very impressed as
I waited for entrance. I had never gone to a home beside the
Queen's palace. This was not my life; *my* life was on the streets,
working with young people. I was from an average, down-to-

earth family. I couldn't help but ask myself, *Ellen, what are you doing, coming to a place like this?*

The flat was on the third floor, in the corner overlooking the palace grounds. Conny, Corrie's secretary, greeted me as I entered the room. Corrie was sitting in a little grey chair, with the sun streaming in through big windows behind her. The view was magnificent and the room very elegant.

We talked a little – just casual conversation in order to get acquainted – and then Conny and I went to the kitchen to make tea. Conny bagan to tell me all of the things that were important to Corrie, such as tea in the mornings, afternoon tea after her nap, and no touches allowed, such as little kisses to show affection or helping her by taking her arm. Conny wanted me to understand how important independence was to Corrie. I began to realize that although Corrie ten Boom looked like a grandmother, she didn't want to be treated like one. Many questions filled my mind.

When we came back from the kitchen, Conny suggested that we sit on the balcony. As soon as we went outside, I felt the wind and knew it was too cool for Corrie. 'Conny,' I said, 'is there not a little wrap for Corrie?' Conny told me some time later that she knew then that I would take care of Corrie, and this made her feel good and quiet inside, knowing that someone else would take over her place and would love and really care for Corrie.

We continued to sit outside for a little while. Corrie then showed me her new manuscript, which was written in German. It was entitled *Marching Orders*. Corrie said, 'You need to read it through and tell me what you think of it.' Read it through? I could read very little German. You can imagine how I felt! I soon discovered, though, that Corrie writes very easy German. The German people call it 'Corrie ten Boom German'. After handing me the manuscript, she said, 'Ellen, I am going to take a little nap.' Conny and her fiancé decided to go for a walk. I was left alone.

I thought to myself: *When the elderly take a nap, it is for at least an hour, so now what do I do?* I sat there with that book manuscript in my hands in a strange apartment, and I didn't even know what a manuscript was. Strange feelings bubbled up in me.

Then, to my surprise, Corrie was back in ten minutes, feeling lively and strong. I expressed my surprise and she answered, 'Ten minutes is all you need when God gives the sleep.' That wasn't like many seventy-five-year-old women I knew!

She asked, 'Have you read it?'

I replied, 'Well, I read one story, and it was very interesting.'

Her eyes sparkled in a way I was to come to know well, and she said, 'Ellen, I am so happy that God is going to give you to me.' I was speechless.

She then started talking with me as if I had already decided to work with her, and I had not! I could see she was writing books and still travelling a great deal – this was the first place she could call home in twenty years – and I became quite certain that I could not help her in any way.

I said, 'I don't think I am the right person. I don't speak English. I cannot speak German very well. Corrie, I cannot type, I cannot drive a car . . .'

There we sat in that beautiful sunny room, birds singing outside, and all I could think about were the negatives. I will never forget what Corrie said next. It was so typical of her. Her face was bright, her eyes sparkling. 'Ellen, I'm happy you know it. You can*not* do it, but God can do it through you.'

I had met the real Corrie, all right, on my very first visit, and she surprised me. I had wanted consoling words. She gave me shocking words. I had expected a kindly grandmother. She was a soldier of the Lord, quite qualified to write a book about *Marching Orders*. I dealt in impossibilities. She seemed to deal with possibilities. Later I was to realize more fully that those words she had spoken were just a preface to many situations where God would have His chance to work because I could not do the task.

4

Lord, Please Help Ellen

I reflected for several days about my meeting with Corrie. I had never met anyone quite like her. My final words to her had been, 'Corrie, I really *can't* do it. You seem sure, but I'm not. I need some clear answers from the Lord.'

To go with Corrie meant a major change in my life's plans, and I had much to consider. She had replied, 'Yes, of course, Ellen. Let us pray about it.' And that's what we did – and what I continued to do in the coming days. I had never really waited upon the Lord and prayed with such intensity. I felt a great fear that I might never get back to Holland to be with my own family. We were not that close, but family is family. I felt as if my decision affected all of us. Then the Lord gave me a Scripture from Acts: ' . . . Believe on the Lord Jesus Christ, and thou shalt be saved, and thy house' (Acts 16:31). In Dutch it reads a little differently, having more to do with the family: ' . . . you shall be saved and your household as well.' God would take care of my family. When I read those words, I knew that God could help me make the right decision for myself and for my family. But other questions arose in my mind.

One had to do with my new home. At this time I was living in a room in the hospital, but the hospital had just arranged for me to have a flat. My brother, an architect, was helping me with the forthcoming move. The new flat excited me; travelling with Corrie ten Boom did not. In fact, I had never spent much time thinking about travelling around the world. I had always thought of going places to *live*, not just to pass through. Wasn't that the way a missionary did it? They put roots down and built churches. They didn't tramp all over the world.

The biggest obstacle, though, was my work at the hospital. I truly loved my job – it was fulfilling and satisfying to me. I knew that I was expected to give at least three months' notice, and Corrie needed someone sooner than that. I prayed an earnest prayer: 'Lord, I need Your guidance. If I am to go with Corrie, I need some miracles. I want to leave the hospital as a child of God, a child of the King of kings. I want to leave in a royal way. I will need first to see the head nurse. I want her to be happy about this and to be an encouragement to me. Every person, Lord, that I must see – from the director on down – I will look to for encouragement and the right counsel. God, only You can open all the doors and make it right. If the doors open, I will be happy. If they don't, I will be happy. Whatever happens, I will know it is You.' I didn't want a reluctant, 'Okay, Ellen, if you must go, go' from my superiors. I wanted their *blessing*. It was a lot to ask.

First I went to my head nurse and told her about Corrie. She said, 'Ellen, I would do it if I were you. You will have so many interesting experiences, and the travel and being with Corrie ten Boom will be the greatest opportunity of your life. Your work as a nurse will not suffer if you work for her a year or two. When you return you will know people all over the world and you will have learned more about other countries. Your outlook on life will be broader, and that is always a good thing.' She reminded me, however, that it was summer and a difficult time to leave the hospital. Again, I was told that three months' notice was expected.

I knew I had to see the Director of the Hospital, but first I went to the Assistant Director. Her name was Ms de Heer, which means 'the Lord' in Dutch. What better name?

Ms 'the Lord' was a good Dutch Reformed woman; sturdy, dependable, with a braid wrapped around her head and heavy brown shoes. She was a warmhearted, solid person. The wind would not blow her away. In a clinic with so many thousands of people, one didn't see Ms de Heer unless one was in trouble or in real need of counsel. I told her my story, and then she looked kindly at me and said, 'Ellen, have you prayed about this?' I assured her I had been doing little else! She then said, 'Let me call the Director and ask if you can see her right away. Three months is our limit, but we will see what happens.'

I left to see the Director, whose name was Ms Vander Weg, which is Ms 'the Way' in Dutch. (A little prophetic, perhaps?) Right away her response was negative. 'Ellen, why would you want to leave your good job? This lady is seventy-five years old. She could die tomorrow, and you would lose your nice job, your social security, all your pension rights . . . '

I thought the ground under my feet was caving in. Then she asked, 'Do you know why this other girl is leaving? Could it be that this Corrie is a very difficult old lady? You never know, Ellen. Older people can be difficult to get along with.'

I sat up quickly and replied, 'Oh, Ms Vander Weg, Conny is leaving because she is getting married.' I told her the name of the doctor who was Conny's fiancé. Now it was Ms Vander Weg's turn to be surprised. She repeated his name and finally said, 'Well, Ellen, that girl must be pure gold, for he is the finest doctor in this hospital. That changes things. All right, Ellen, I will work on it and see what can be done about an early release.'

I left her office with mixed feelings. I had little doubt about my decision – the answers to my prayer had come too quickly and forcefully for me to doubt. I could see God pushing me out. I still didn't really want to leave, but my peace came in knowing that God was in control. I phoned Corrie to tell her what had happened.

But Corrie already knew. 'Yes, Ellen,' she said. 'The Lord confirmed it to me. I was positive that you would be coming to help me.'

Help me – those words again. But this time I had to look heavenward and pray, 'And Lord, please help Ellen!'

5

A Faster Pace

So how did I begin my great adventure as a secretary and
travelling companion to Corrie ten Boom? By travelling to an
exotic foreign country and ministering to poor and suffering
people? Hardly. I took driving lessons.

That is no small or common task in Holland. Many people
in Holland get around all their lives by walking and riding
bicycles or motor scooters. It was nothing extraordinary for me
to ride my bicycle ten miles a day when I was taking my home
economics course as a teenager. If I had to make a trip of more
than twenty-five miles, I'd take a bus or train. I loved the relaxed freedom and simplicity of open-air transportation, and
our public transport system is very reliable. Cars seemed very
complicated and driving a great responsibility. Besides that,
driving lessons and cars are expensive in Holland, and the
driving test is very difficult. Many people find that it takes
them many months, even years, to get a driving licence. Suddenly I had a job that required me to drive a car, and I had less
than three months to learn how to drive and to get a licence.
What a surprise that Corrie gave me the money to take the
lessons. I began immediately.

The day finally came to take the test. I had been taking
lessons with two girls who were super drivers. We went together to take the test and we all passed the written portion
without any trouble. Then came the driving test. My fellow

students preceded me – and to my surprise, both of them failed! I felt terrible for them – and even more nervous for myself. I prayed a Corrie prayer: 'Lord, I can't do it, but You *can*!'

A friend had also come with me, and the last words I heard as I got into the examiner's car were: 'I'll be praying the whole time.'

I had been warned that the examiner was a stern, severe man. After a short drive he began to ask me questions. My application showed that I was changing my career, and he asked about that. I told him about Corrie. Then he began asking questions about healing and God. It was rush hour, and I had to look out for so many things – bicycles can always take you by surprise! I thought it very strange that he would want to talk about the Lord, instead of letting me concentrate on turning at the corners!

Finally I said, 'Sir, I can only do one thing at a time. Driving requires my full attention, otherwise I will not pass the test. I need to pass, Sir, and I must concentrate. Could we just wait and talk *after* the test?'

He answered, 'No. You are a better driver than you think.' We then went to a less-congested part of town, where it was easier for me to talk and drive at the same time. I continued to tell him about the Lord, and he continued to give me orders about where to turn and what to do.

I knew all the while that at the end of the test I had to reverse into a parking bay. I knew that might also be the end of some of the parked cars! When we got to the car park, however, all the places were filled, and my examiner said, 'There is no need to do this part. Just drive over to that little bridge and park. I have learned more about healing and God. This will be the last time we see each other.' He did not even give me time to tell him that I could not park very well backwards. Suddenly he became severe and stern-looking again, and by the tone of his voice, I feared the worst.

Silently we walked back into the building and I waited with my friend. At last they called my name. I had passed! The first time! It was a miracle. Although it was a dull, rainy day, for me the sun was shining. And yet I knew, deep within, God had helped me do it – not I in my own strength.

When I returned to Corrie's flat with the good news, we almost danced for joy, but settled instead for a time of praise and a little cake and coffee. Three hours later Corrie said, 'Ellen, there is a good film showing in Utrecht, and I would like to see it. You know that city well since you lived there, so let's go.'

Very often when God gives us an opportunity or a gift, He also gives us challenges and tests, so we can learn the value of our gift and continue to trust in Him. This was my first challenge in driving after I had earned my licence.

I had never driven a car by myself – an instructor or a friend had always been beside me, telling me what to do. And driving in the dark just added to the challenge. With some encouraging words we left for Utrecht. The streets seemed terribly narrow, and every time a car passed us, I felt sure we would end up against a tree. We had a little Volkswagen, but it seemed as wide as a Cadillac that night. Still busy conquering my fears, I looked to the right, and there was Corrie, sleeping soundly. Her trust in my driving helped me to do my very best and not be afraid. Maybe that is exactly what the Master had in mind when He fell asleep during that stormy night so long ago.

Corrie became a very precious load to me, and each time I saw her drive away with another person, I couldn't help but worry a little. One afternoon she left with another driver and told me she would be back by 6 p.m. Six o'clock came . . . and then seven . . . and eight . . . and nine. The phone rang with news that Corrie was in the hospital. She had, indeed, been in a road accident. I hurried to the hospital and was relieved to find that only her shoulder was broken and her arm was fractured in five places. (I had expected much worse!) She was badly shaken up and painfully bruised.

Following the accident, Corrie had to be in the hospital for nine weeks, and we both learned one more of God's reasons for helping me to pass the driving test the first time. If I had not passed the test I would not have been able to visit Corrie daily in the hospital, for the hospital was about eighty miles away.

Corrie was an impatient hospital patient, but that was not difficult to understand. She is such an energetic person, with so much she wants to do. And there she was, stuck in a bed, unable to use her right arm and hand. She couldn't write, bathe herself, or wash and brush her hair. I came every day to be with her, and we would work and talk about the news of the day. Going to and from the hospital, I got lots of practice in driving by myself, both day and night.

The last night before Corrie was to be released from the hospital, something happened that was to prove to be a testing time. Knowing Corrie would be going home with me the next day, I carefully packed her suitcase – the underclothing she would need, a dress, her coat. It had started to snow a little, and before I left for the hospital, our neighbour, Mrs van der Hoeven, called to say, 'Ellen, the weather is not the best, and the streets are icy. It is really quite terrible. Are you sure you should go?'

Without hesitation I replied, 'But you know Corrie needs me. This is the last night for her in the hospital. It's such a big event for her. If I don't come, she will be disappointed.'

Before reaching the main highway to Arnhem, I had to drive at least thirty miles, through many little villages. After almost nine weeks of driving those narrow, curving roads, I had come to know all the houses, farms, shops, and turns and dips in the road quite well. But this night my eyes had to be constantly on the road, for it was becoming very slippery. I thought often about the call from Mrs van der Hoeven. John 15:13 also came to my mind: 'Greater love hath no man than this, that a man lay down his life for his friends.' And through those first three months, Corrie had become my friend. I had become deeply interested in her life goals and more committed than ever to help her as much as possible.

Near the main highway was a section of road with a ditch on one side and farmland on the other. Past the ditch was a large cement wall. Although I was not driving fast and I knew the way, when I reached that point, the car started to spin around in circles out of control on the ice! Every time my car went to the left side of the road, a car would pass on the right, and though my car spun several times, no other car was hit. I didn't know what to do to try to regain control of that little Volkswagen on the ice. Finally the nose of the car smashed into the cement wall and the car dropped into the mud in the ditch. The car was a total loss, damaged beyond repair, but somehow I came out of that car in an instant. I found myself standing on the side of the road, with the keys in one hand and Corrie's suitcase in the other.

Two navy boys came along right at the moment and were astonished to see me standing there with the car crumpled in the ditch. I have always believed that God sent angels to take care of me. I was bruised and had a concussion, but I was able to walk to a nearby garage. A friend came to take me to the home of his parents. They called the hospital and told Corrie what had happened and promised her that they would bring her home from the hospital the next day.

Several days later I was driven to where Corrie had been taken. I was not allowed to walk, and Corrie was too weak to be up the whole day, so we both ended up in bed! During the first few days the Lord sent wonderful people to help us, but a week later, Corrie and I found ourselves alone. During those long winter days, wanting to break up the hours, we started to have coffee at 11 a.m. and a cup of tea and perhaps a biscuit or cookie at 3 p.m. With no one to help us, we put our weaknesses together: Corrie boiled the water, put some biscuits on a serving dish, and I made the tea. We often used these times each day to pray, read a book aloud, or share our thoughts, so I asked Tante Corrie to read James 5. I had been praying for healing every day since the accident, and others had done the same for me, but my head still seemed strange and my body ached. Reading this passage in James about healing, we recognized that we had done everything except pray for each other. I had been selfishly concentrating on my own needs, and had failed to pray diligently for others. The Lord used this passage in James to point this out to me. I don't remember how long I prayed that afternoon, but I felt compelled to pray for many people who I knew needed God's help. And the Lord did what He promised in His Word: The next day I could do the work that was expected of me, with a clear head and greater strength.

In just a short period of time I had learned how God can give us great opportunities and very personal miracles – and how He also gives us challenges and tests to teach us even deeper lessons about His love for us and His purposes in our lives. When we prepare and ask His help, He helps us pass the exams of this life. When we practise and are careful – but then hit icy patches in life, when we don't know what to do – He takes care of us and even turns these tragedies into good lessons. I had discovered that God had very definite reasons for giving this bicycle-loving Dutch girl two more wheels to drive and a faster-paced life!

6

Helping

After the accident with the Volkswagen, we were without a car for the rest of the winter. When spring came, we began to pray for a new car. We were concerned that the car be roomy and quiet enough so Corrie could truly rest as we travelled between speaking engagements. We also needed a car big enough to carry all the books we took with us. Corrie went with the pastor of our church to shop for a car, and she finally chose a green Renault. She asked the dealer to drive her to the roughest road in the area, so she could test the shock absorbers, but before they left, she shocked the dealer by saying, 'Before you start, let's pray and ask the Lord to bless the car.' Corrie always used even little opportunities to share her big message about God's love.

Corrie would never buy anything unless she could pay cash. She felt paying cash made it easier for her to know God's will, for if the money was not there, she knew her desire for the thing would pass. In this case, the money came just at the necessary moment.

So the car was comfortable enough, and she could afford it – but Corrie had one big worry. She was concerned that the car looked too nice – much too nice for an evangelist tramp named Corrie ten Boom. She especially didn't like the chrome strips on the sides, which prevented the car from being easily scratched. She felt that those strips would cause people to

35

think that she was a millionaire, and that would not be for
God's glory.

The dealer asked her, 'Shall I take all of those strips off and
make it dull?'

Corrie thought for a moment and said to me, 'Ellen, that
would look strange, too, would it not?'

'Ya, Tante Corrie,' I had to reply, 'that would look strange.'

'We will buy the car with the strips on,' she said.

I understood what Corrie was *not* saying. The strips on the
side of the car looked showy to her, but she was also concerned
that she would appear to have false humility if she asked the
dealer to remove them.

Years later, when we no longer travelled so extensively by
car, Corrie gave the Renault to a family with five children. She
felt they needed the roominess of the larger car more than we
did. Corrie purchased a smaller grey car for us.

The people expected her to *look* like a missionary. Deep
within her own self, I don't think appearance mattered one
way or another. She felt very secure in her own self and had no
need for fancy clothing, cosmetics, or material things to make
her feel better about herself. When I started to work with her,
she mostly wore inexpensive, colourless dresses and heavy, big
black shoes. After all, it didn't matter what she wore to speak
in leper colonies, prisons, and mission stations in Africa, India,
and other parts of the world. Once she spoke to a group of
women who were the wives of leaders of nations from around
the world, and she wore a cardigan, jumper and skirt that were
of conflicting shades of blue. Styles just didn't matter to her.
She had one goal, and that was reaching those leaders' wives
for Jesus.

I could see, however, that clothing is important to some
women, and mismatched or poor clothing can actually be a
stumbling stone that keeps them from fully hearing the Gospel.
I believe God wants us to look as attractive as possible, because we represent Him. Jesus told us that the messenger was
'the first word of His message. If they receive you.' He said,
'they receive Me.' (*See* Matthew 10:40.) Our appearance

should complement our message, since we represent Christ. We are to be 'representatives fair' for the Lord. Corrie was so busy representing the Lord that she had no time to be concerned about her appearance, and I felt that this was one area where I could help her 'beyond a cup of tea'. I just didn't know how to begin.

I didn't have long to be concerned, though, because even those big black shoes had to be replaced occasionally, and one day we set out for the shoe shop where Corrie always bought her shoes. She had gone to this shop in Haarlem, her hometown, for years, and no one had ever suggested she buy a different style. Practical woman that she was, Corrie figured black went with everything. The day we went she had on a light blue dress, quite a contrast to the heavy grey suit that she wore when she spoke. The blue made her skin look almost translucent. I didn't say anything when the man brought out the big black shoes, but when she put them on, I said 'Tante Corrie, shall we ask the man if he has these same shoes in a different colour – maybe beige?'

'A blue dress and beige shoes would look nice,' she said. 'Do you have them in beige?'

'Yes, and in brown, too.'

We walked out of the store with different-coloured shoes for Tante Corrie, and before the day was over, we had added a number of other new items to her wardrobe. In the process, Corrie discovered a little more about a world that had always seemed strange and tiring to her. She also discovered anew that shops have shopkeepers who need to hear about Jesus, too!

Over the months I learned what Corrie would and would not wear, and she trusted me to do her shopping. The dresses had to have a belt, a comfortable neckline for speaking, and preferably a jacket. I truly enjoy shopping, and visiting the stores was fun for me. It was a change of pace and an opportunity to see what was happening in the community. Many times while I was shopping, God would let me begin a conversation with a saleslady – many of them would ask why a tall young woman was looking through racks of clothes designed for short, older women! We would talk about Corrie, and very soon we would be talking about the Lord.

In all, Corrie was relieved that she didn't have to worry about the shopping. Now she had more becoming clothes to wear. And I had a new way to help her that I thoroughly enjoyed.

I learned yet another lesson: when God calls us alongside someone to help them, very often the helping chores are ones we truly enjoy. He wants us to have fun in His service. He blends our talents with those of others, so that each of us does what we do best and what we enjoy doing the most.

7

Hungarian Miracle

I was lacking a very basic secretarial skill when I came to work
with Corrie: I couldn't type. I'll never forget one man I met at
Conny's wedding reception, who asked me quite bluntly,
'Why are *you* going to be Corrie's companion and secretary, if
you don't speak English and you don't know how to type?'

I did not understand at that time how subtle Satan is. The
enemy of our souls never misses an opportunity to instil doubt
in our minds about our weaknesses. Often the enemy uses even
well-meaning people. This man meant me no harm; he only
had Corrie's best interests in mind. But for a moment, a dark
shadow crossed my path. I could not even give him an answer.
I just stood there with my doubts, looking around at the
garden and the wedding guests. My eyes spotted Corrie, and
the words she had used the first time we met came back to me
again: 'You cannot, but God can do it through you.'

With two fingers, I began to learn to type. Gradually, I began to discover just what it is that a secretary does. One of my
first assignments was to fill in the papers needed for a visa that
would allow me to go to Hungary with Corrie.

With this assignment came many other thoughts – sometimes scary ones. I had never flown before, and we were
scheduled to fly to Hungary. I had never been behind the Iron
Curtain. But the more I thought about the trip, the more I
focused on the people we might meet. God gave me a great

burden for them, and I began praying for them and for God to
direct and bless our time there.

One morning while at the breakfast table, Corrie and I
began to discuss our trip to Hungary – the places we would go,
some of the people we would meet. The Hungarians, like the
Dutch, had suffered much during the war years, but the rebuilding process had been slower. The Hungarian government
continued to have close ties with the Soviet Union, and re-
ligious groups in the country were still rigidly controlled.
Corrie had visited Hungary in 1964, and she was eager to
return to this land where she had found so much hunger for
the Word. I knew it would be a great privilege if my visa was
approved and I was allowed to go with her.

Corrie and I often used those breakfast-table times to talk
about our plans for the future. I had learned very quickly that
Corrie always makes big plans. Even though she was seventy-
five, her plans were young and fresh. When Corrie was just a
child, one of her friends asked how many plans she had for her
life, and Corrie said, 'I have twenty,' and she started to count
them. Her little friend had laughed, but Corrie went right on
down the list, until she had told her all of them. Then Corrie
had asked her friend, 'How many do you have? Two or three?
You see, if only half of my twenty plans come to pass, or even
a quarter, I will still have accomplished more plans than you.'
That has always been Corrie's attitude, and it is still the way
she approaches life. She makes great big, faith-stretching
plans, which allow her faith in a working God to be tested.

While we were talking that morning of our plans for
Hungary, the travel agency called and asked to speak to Corrie.
A similar call a few days earlier had informed me that my visa
for Hungary had been granted. We assumed this call would
bring more good news. I remember vividly how Corrie put the
telephone back on the hook and quietly said, 'Ellen, plans are
changing. My visa has been refused.' She sat down and lifted
her hands up to Jesus, as if she was holding the visa-request
papers in them, and said, 'Lord, Jesus, I don't understand
this. You gave me the desire to go back to the people in this

country, and now I am refused. I give this refusal to You as a little bit of material for You to build a miracle.' And with that, she closed her prayer. Immediately she began to read her mail and to make other plans.

I was puzzled. My visa had been granted: why not Corrie's? Should we try again? Had I made a mistake? Had I failed somehow? I had felt so burdened for these people and had prayed so much. What had happened?

Corrie saw my perplexity and how bad I felt, and she said, 'Ellen, *we have a working God*. Do you remember the verse from 1 Corinthians 15:58 I gave you the first day you came to be with me? "Therefore, be ye stedfast, unmoveable, always abounding in the work of the Lord, forasmuch as ye know that your labour is not in vain in the Lord." Come now, tomorrow is another day, and we have a meeting. Let us make plans!'

The next day we travelled to Groningen, where Corrie spoke to a large audience. I watched her closely, to see if the disappointment about the visa would affect her speaking, but it didn't. Corrie gave a beautiful message on our need to be prepared to meet Jesus at any time, and I saw the people draw closer to Jesus as the Holy Spirit took Corrie's words and moved among the listeners. The meetings were always followed by a time for counselling, and I went to the pastor's study with a group of young people that night and forgot all about the visa and not being able to go to Hungary. The next days were busy with the follow-up work from the meeting, and it was only occasionally that a dark cloud would loom on the horizon of my thinking. I would ask forgiveness for my doubting, but I still could not fully understand why God would give us such a great burden for Hungary and yet deny us the privilege of going there to minister.

About a week later our mailman delivered an unusual parcel. It was neatly wrapped and covered with foreign stamps and inspection stickers. It was postmarked Budapest, Hungary. What could it be? I quickly got a pair of scissors, and after cutting through all the tape, Corrie unfolded the paper. We could not believe our eyes. In the packet were five copies of

Corrie's book, *A Prisoner and Yet* – in Hungarian! And published by Hungarians! No communist country was publishing evangelistic books, yet a little note with the books told us that 1,000 of these books had been printed. When Corrie had visited the country before, she had made friends with some people who apparently had spent the last three years making the complicated arrangements to have Corrie's book printed in an official way. A thousand books may not seem very many to westerners, but behind the Iron Curtain, books are read and reread many times. They don't sit on shelves, but are passed around from family to family as quickly as possible. Sometimes they are even recopied by hand – so there is no telling how many copies now exist or how many people have read that book.

I looked at Corrie and said, 'Tante Corrie, isn't this even better than a return trip to Hungary?'

She looked at me and then heavenward. 'Ya, Ellen, it is better.'

No trip to Hungary, or visits with the brothers and sisters there. But in my imagination I could see thousands of outstretched hands receiving a book, and within it, a great message about God's love. The Lord had responded to my clouds of doubt with a shower of His blessings – not just a few drops – but a shower! He knew that only a shower would help His child Ellen to trust Him more and drive the doubts away.

We often cry out of pain, but that morning I shed some tears out of joy. Our working God had not closed the door to Hungary – He had just opened a *different* door in answering our prayers and releasing our burden.

8

Paying Bills

In the beginning of our work, I felt a bit apprehensive every time Corrie would say, 'The Lord told me we have to go . . . ' or 'the Lord told me to do . . . '

I thought, *What a great thing, for a Christian to be able to know what the Lord wants him to do*. I prayed often that the Lord would also tell *me* where He wanted us to go, because I never seemed to hear His voice like Corrie did. Finally I realized that the Lord had called me to help, and not to lead, and that obedience to my calling was all that He asked of me. He didn't need me to hear, He just needed me to be willing to follow Corrie and help her in any way that I could. It took me a while to understand my role, but when I did, the Lord blessed me with a deep peace. We often have to do things that we don't like.

Often I felt like Ruth following Naomi around the world, saying 'I will go where you go, lodge where you lodge, your people shall be my people, and your God my God' (*see* Ruth 1:16). I must admit, though, that sometimes it was difficult to follow – especially when it meant a change in my approach to money.

I was accustomed to a regular salary in my work as a nurse. I felt I earned my money and I could spend it as I wanted. Suddenly I was put into a position of trusting for money. I had to pray that the Lord would meet our needs, and then when we received money, I had to pray that we would spend it as *He* wanted it spent. What a different way to approach finances!

I shall never forget our first trip to Russia. Corrie felt we should go for three weeks, and I was astounded when the travel office told us how much a three-week trip to Russia would cost. We didn't have that kind of money, and I didn't know how the Lord would supply it. Corrie and I prayed each day for the trip – and for the money to come in. We had only three weeks before we were to depart, and after the first week, not a penny had come in.

Then Corrie surprised me by saying, 'Ellen, we need to give 2000 of our guilders [about £475] to another organization. They need it, and the Lord spoke to me quite clearly to give it to them.'

Her voice had a slight question in it, though, and I quickly said, 'But Tante Corrie, *we* need that money for Russia.' Here we were planning a trip and didn't have nearly enough money and Corrie was going to give away what we did have?

'Well,' she replied hesitantly, 'perhaps it is not right to give it away.'

But two days later she walked into my bedroom, one corner of which was our little office. She sat down resolutely. 'Ellen,' she said, 'God made it very clear we *have* to send the money. Here is the cheque. Please type the envelope and take it to the post office.'

I could see that she had no doubt that this is what the Lord wanted her to do and that she had a great peace about giving away our guilders. I took the envelope and cheque with the other mail to the post office. That afternoon the heavenly Father surprised us. In looking through our mail we found a letter from an American publishing company that wanted to published *The Hiding Place*. With the letter was a prepayment for the manuscript – *exactly* the amount we needed for our mission to Russia! As it turned out, another company later bought the rights to the book, and we had to repay this money, so we really had two miracles. The money came at just the right time for the trip to Russia, and then again, enough money came at just the time to repay the publishers. Never again did I question Corrie when she felt the Lord directing her to give away some of her money.

During the years I worked with Corrie, we lived by a principle of never asking for money. Corrie had learned that lesson from her sister Betsie. Betsie had said to Corrie while they were in the concentration camp, 'We will travel all over the world, and there will always be enough money. The Father in heaven will provide.'

At one time, Corrie had many obligations, and she told the audience what her needs were. The message had been about giving ourselves to the Lord, the need of conversion – to be born again. After the meeting a woman came to her and said, 'I have a large sum of money here. Do you need it?'

Corrie was quiet for a moment and then she said, 'Did the *Lord* tell you to do this? Are you willing to give yourself to the Lord?'

The woman answered, 'Do you need the money? Yes or no?' Corrie's answer was no. The woman left the room very upset.

Then Corrie saw what was happening. Money had become a part of the message. She had told the people about the love of Jesus and His forgiveness, but somehow money had become wedged into the minds of the people and they were responding to her needs, instead of to the Lord. Corrie was very troubled by this realization. The Lord had given her the strength not to accept the woman's money, and she went to her room and prayed.

'Lord,' Corrie said, 'money comes between the message. What must I do?'

'From now on, never ask for money!' was God's answer.

That same week her sister, Nollie, and a good trustworthy friend both wrote to her, telling her that the Lord had told them Corrie should never ask for money. For Corrie, that was a real confirmation of the Lord's desire.

From that time on, Corrie would pray when she needed money: 'Father, You own the cattle on a thousand hills. Could you please sell a cow and give me the money?' And when the Father thought that it was good for His child Corrie to have the money, He would send it to her. How special was the cheque that came from a farmer who wrote: 'We somehow felt impressed to sell some of our cows and send you the money!'

Throughout all her years of ministry, Corrie never had a lawyer. She trusted God that all financial matters would turn out for the best. If someone didn't pay a bill, Corrie would pray that God would use that unpaid money to win souls through some other channel. If someone didn't play fair with her, Corrie would pray for that person and forgive him.

We were visiting with Catherine Marshall at the time Corrie was deciding if *The Hiding Place* should be made into a film. We discussed author's rights with Catherine, and she asked Corrie, 'Don't you have a lawyer?'

'No,' Corrie responded. 'It is much easier to trust God than to trust people. He is my lawyer.' That was her attitude about all financial and legal matters. The money was not hers – it was His – and she trusted God to take care of His own resources.

9

Getting Acquainted

The nine weeks that Corrie was hospitalized after her road accident were trying ones in many ways. I had just started working with Corrie and had many questions about what I was expected to do and *not* to do. I think sometimes we Christians tend to think that we are all to act alike and be cheerful and full of joy and faith all the time. During these weeks I learned a little more about Corrie ten Boom and the traits that make her an *individual*, a one-of-a-kind person.

While Corrie was in the hospital, her book *Marching Orders for the End Battle* was printed. In it, she reminds readers that we must be strong in difficult times.

Corrie felt very helpless and dependent in the hospital – which is difficult for a woman who is accustomed to being helpful and independent. One day I came to her room to find a young Jewish girl, Margalit van Zuiden, sitting beside Corrie's bed. Corrie would call Margalit a 'completed Jew', because she had fallen in love with the Jewish Rabbi, Jesus of Nazareth. Margalit was studying to become a registered nurse, and she was sharing with Corrie the things she was learning. Corrie looked rather troubled. It was sunny that day and after awhile, we all sat quietly and tried to enjoy the sunshine. Then Corrie said, 'You know, something is bothering me very much, and I don't know what to do. I have just finished rereading my own book *Marching Orders for the End Battle*. I am encouraging others to be strong, but I am not strong and victorious myself. I feel weak and defeated here in this hospital. I am ashamed.'

'Tante Corrie,' Margalit responded, 'I was so blessed through one of Oswald Chambers' writings. He made it clear that we must not try to live up to our own testimony, but that we have to stay close to Jesus.'

Instantly the look on Corrie's face changed. There was a release, and after a time of prayer, Corrie wanted to sit up a little straighter in the bed. I washed her face and hands, combed her hair, and suddenly we found ourselves looking into those sparkling blue eyes again. Corrie had accepted that young girl's words as from the Lord, and it changed her countenance and her attitude immediately.

I saw this happen many times in the years that followed. It did not matter *who* was speaking – a young Christian or a well-known Christian personality, poor or rich, educated or uneducated. Corrie did not depend on *who* was speaking. She heard *what* was being said and the spirit in which it was being given. And she was quick to discern when the Holy Spirit was prompting someone to speak.

Another time Corrie was quite upset about the way Christians could be involved in what she thought were non-Christian activities. She was talking to Cliff Barrows (of the Billy Graham team) about it. Cliff has been, through all the years, like a big brother to us, and having seen his steady walk with the Lord, it was easy to talk with him about this. He said, 'Corrie, God gave us energy to fulfil the Great Commission. If we keep on fulfilling our call we will make people thirsty for the Gospel. Our task is not to judge other Christians.' Corrie took his advice to heart and heard the Lord correcting her attitude through Cliff's words. She was not too proud or too stubborn to hear something from the Lord through another person.

Down through the months and years, I learned to know Corrie as another human being. To me she was a woman filled with human traits and sometimes human flaws. It often amazed us both that many people thought of her as being *already perfect.* I remember so well some guests who spent a night with us in Holland. They were very tense at being in the same house with Corrie ten Boom. They thought Corrie to be very pious and holy, and figured she must spend much of the night hours praying and reading her Bible. What a surprise when it came time for bed and Corrie said, 'Now do you have anything to tell me? If so, do it quickly; otherwise, I'll be asleep!'

One of the young girls asked me quietly, 'Ellen, what will I do if I oversleep tomorrow morning? What will Corrie say?' I told her not to worry, that Corrie also enjoyed sleeping longer now and then. The next day at breakfast she whispered to me. 'Ellen, Corrie didn't get up at five.'

I said, 'No. What are you thinking? Do you think we get up that early?'

'Yes,' she answered. 'I thought Corrie would get up at five and kneel down and pray and wrestle with the Lord. But do you know what she was doing instead, Ellen?'

I knew what Corrie more than likely was doing, but I wanted to hear it from her.

'Oh, Ellen,' she said with great surprise, 'she was *snoring*!'

We all laughed about it later, when we shared that news with Corrie. 'That is the joy of being at ease with Jesus,' Corrie said. She has a natural way of living and a great sense of humour. If needed, she *did* get up at 5 a.m. to read and study. But if not, she slept.

I remember the day we received a letter from a woman who told us that she had named her little bulldog 'Corrie ten Boom'. I saw the twinkle in Corrie's eye. Instead of being affronted that a dog had been named after her, she loved the idea. She carried a picture of that dog with her for some time, and would sometimes bark in imitation of her namesake!

In looking back over the years, several outstanding traits about Corrie stand out in my mind. The first is that she has a great determination. I remember so well the days after Corrie had come home from the hospital and she was unable to use her right hand. First she was discouraged, for she felt she had a lot to write – too many ideas were not yet on paper. But the discouragement quickly turned into action. One day she went to a bookstore to buy a writing booklet – the kind first-graders use. She had decided to start all over again and learn to write with her left hand. Every day she would sit at her desk, copying her ABCs with a great effort, until she thought she had done them the right way. She also began to use a tape recorder more. Before that, Corrie had never needed to dictate, because she could write nearly as fast as her quick mind worked.

In addition to her writing exercises, she exercised with weights. A friend made a bar with a bag of sand on it, and many times a day Corrie would stop to lift that bar. I gave her a massage every day, and she exercised her fingers in hot water. She would play the piano to exercise her fingers, and I'll never forget the day that she could once again reach an octave. Corrie didn't give up – not even at seventy-five. She refused to give in to her accident or her age.

Another trait that I quickly saw in Corrie was that she is a masterful storyteller – mainly because she never takes it for granted that everyone in the room has made a real commitment to Jesus. Corrie focuses her stories on the Gospel and aims them at people who might not know the Lord. That way, although she tells the same stories over and over, they stay fresh and they reach hearts.

At one point Corrie thought she might quit telling the torch story, in which she compares a person without Jesus to a torch without batteries. Even a child can understand sin and the Cross when Corrie tells the story of the torch. It is probably her best-known story. She uses simple language, and nobody has to guess at her meaning. I saw many people in the audiences who responded to its message and also saw some who *expected* the story and brought their friends just to hear it. So I encouraged Corrie to continue to tell the story.

Even though Corrie told the same story over and over, she would prepare thoroughly for each message. She filled many notebooks over the years by writing and rewriting her messages. While she wrote, she prayed and asked the Lord to help choose the right words and select the right stories to share with a particular audience. Often the Lord would show her new truths in her old stories, so each time, she came away from her preparation time refreshed in the Lord and ready to tell a story as if she had never told it before.

After a meeting she would pray, 'Lord, bless every word that You spoke through me and cleanse every word I spoke that was wrong and take away any bad results.' She changed the wording of her prayer sometimes, but never the meaning nor intent.

She would sometimes be frustrated after a meeting, feeling that she had not done her best. I learned very early in my work with Corrie about when to criticize her message. We were on the train from Alkmaar to Utrecht, and we were discussing all that God had done during her meeting that evening. I was accustomed to reporting things I saw in my patients immediately to my supervisor in the hospital and to freely giving my opinion about patients, so I adopted this same procedure with Corrie. I did not realize that for a speaker, the time right after the message is the most sensitive time. It is then that the speaker is doubting his own ability and that his faith is the weakest. After I had told Corrie all I did not like about the service, she said, 'Ellen, I like it that you listen closely and you want to help me, but could you please wait with the criticism until the next day? Now is the time to build up my faith and to talk about the parts of the meeting that blessed us both.'

I soon learned that the best thing I could do during a service was to listen in the same way that Corrie spoke – as if I were hearing the story for the first time. That way I could be an encouragement to her and God seemed to give me new insights into her stories, too. Often I would single out people in the audience and pray for them as she spoke.

I think Corrie's most powerful illustration of the Cross is a story from the concentration-camp days. Corrie tells how all of the women in the camp had to stand naked in the icy cold before the eyes of the guards. It was during that time that Corrie fully understood the Cross – how terrible it was and how cruel for Jesus to have to hang before all the world in His suffering. When Jesus went to the Cross, they took His garments, He hung there naked. Through her suffering Corrie understood a fraction of Jesus' suffering, and it made her feel so thankful. I don't know how many hundreds of times I have heard Corrie tell that story, yet each time, it brings tears to my eyes.

I remember a special time when Corrie told that story to a group of prisoners. I was sure they would enjoy it – but for all the wrong reasons. How wonderful to see a tenderness and a deep respect for Corrie come over the faces of those men as they began to see the story of the Cross in a new way; they felt that Corrie understood their own shame of prison life, and many were blessed that evening. The greatest encouragement I could give Corrie was to say, 'Tante Corrie, you brought the Cross of Jesus to the people tonight.'

She would look up at me and say, 'Then it is good.' Her stories had just one purpose – to lift up Jesus.

Corrie often needed my reassurance and presence in other ways and at other times. Some of my most special memories are of the early morning hours we spent together, sitting with a cup of tea and biscuit, reading the Bible, and praying over each request that had been mailed to her. I remember one night when I awoke to find the light on in her bedroom. I went in and noticed that she appeared quite frightened. She said, 'I have been unable to sleep.'

'That's okay,' I said. 'I'll just make us some hot chocolate.' I brought my pillow, and we sat in bed together, reading the Word and talking until she went back to sleep. It was a comfort to her just to have me nearby.

10

At Ease With Jesus

Another trait that I grew to recognize and appreciate in Corrie was the great joy she received from giving presents to others.

Corrie never liked trouser-suits. At times, however, I felt rather uncomfortable in a dress, especially when we were in circles where almost everyone else was wearing slacks. I remember Billie Barrows, Cliff Barrows's wife, telling Corrie one day that I needed a trouser-suit for my work with young people and that slacks could be so comfortable. I was happy to hear Billie's opinion – it made me feel better about wearing those that I owned.

On Christmas Eve that year, I could not believe my eyes when Corrie handed me a package and out of the lovely wrapping rolled a beautiful blue trouser-suit! Corrie still doesn't like trouser-suits, and I think she is very happy they are not as popular today, but she was big enough to try to understand others, and in this case, it was her Ellen.

On our very first Christmas together we were recovering from colds, and we had not been able to shop as we had wanted. That year I received the most interesting package I have ever received from Corrie. My present was wrapped in the newspaper from the day before and tied with a red ribbon. That was something that the hippies would have done in those days, or people very involved in ecology. Inside were two small water-colours. To Corrie, the fun was in the love that went with giving and receiving – more than in the gift itself – and the wrapping was unimportant.

When Corrie came to visit us at the time of Peter John's dedication, we gave her a Dutch-looking bouquet of flowers. I knew she would appreciate the flowers – not for the flowers themselves, but because of the love they represented. The next afternoon we heard that our neighbour had come home from the hospital after a heart operation, and I had no time to get something special for him. I asked Corrie, 'Tante Corrie, do you mind if we give away some of your flowers?'

I could tell by the look on her face that nothing could please her more! She had enjoyed the love in which the flowers were given to her, and now she had the double joy of seeing someone else feel that love. Corrie often passed on gifts that people gave to her, especially boxes of candy. She appreciated the love and then felt even better when she could turn right around and give the love to someone else.

One of her friends, a missionary in Mexico City, knew about this habit and gave Corrie a purse that had Corrie's name on it. She said, 'This is really *just for you*, and I want to be sure that you keep it!'

As much as Corrie likes to give presents, she also enjoys good music and parties. I could really share those enjoyments with her!

I grew up surrounded by good music. Mother wanted each of her children to learn to play a musical instrument or to take voice lessons. We girls went to the children's choir at church, and I soon found out that I would never become a great singer! I learned to play the guitar instead. I would have loved to sing, but as a child I don't think I could have handled the tensions of rehearsal and performance; I would have been so nervous that I could not have sung a note.

My sister, Ronnie, sang very well, and she and mother went to choir together. The great day came when Papa took all of us children to hear the results of their rehearsals. Mahler's *Eighth Symphony* was to be performed in Rotterdam, and we were instructed to sit very quietly. The programmes were made out of paper that didn't make a sound when the pages were turned.

After all of the stories I had heard about the choir director, I could hardly wait to see him. His white head punctuated every change in the mood and tempo of the music, and I was totally absorbed by it all. I left the concert with a tremendous headache because I had concentrated so hard.

We went often to organ concerts in the Wilhelmina Kerk. That church was very cold, but we never seemed to notice. One Saturday afternoon while Feike Astma was playing the beautiful organ there, a tremendous thunderstorm interrupted the concert and lightning struck the organ. For a second everything stopped and no person moved, and then the concert went on as if nothing had happened. The roof began to leak, but the audience members just put up their umbrellas and didn't move. We all loved the music that much. It was a special privilege.

When I began working with Corrie, I learned that she loved classical music, too, and Elizabeth van Heemstra's record collection was used often, when we lived in her apartment for a time. Corrie plays the piano and had been raised in a home filled with good music and family singing.

In the beginning of my work with Corrie, I made the mistake of whistling along with the music. Corrie would come to wherever I was to tell me to stop the whistling, saying that I was destroying the music. How embarrassed I was at such moments! I soon realized that Bach was especially sacred to her. When she had arrived back in Holland after the concentration-camp experience, she was hospitalized, and after the nurses had prepared a good meal for her and she was resting in a clean white bed, the radio began to play Bach music. She couldn't do anything else but cry. Even today, I think of Corrie when I hear J. S. Bach's music. During the times when Corrie was not feeling well, I would help her freshen up and dress in her pretty pyjamas, blue and pink with ruffles, and we would sit together and read the Bible with good Bach music on the stereo in the background.

Close to her love for music was her appreciation for parties and festive times. Conny was an excellent hostess. She taught me many things about keeping a conversation going. Group conversation was an art with her, and I had fun watching. After dinner Conny would begin to ask Corrie questions and encourage her to tell stories. She had just the knack for asking Corrie to tell the stories that would minister to the needs of the others in the room. She was sensitive to their needs and thoroughly familiar with Corrie's life, so she could help bring the two together. I tried to follow Conny's example.

Often when we had missionaries visiting us, Corrie would walk out of the room in a special way that let me know she was going to get some gifts for the others. She would come back with books or presents – and write a personal message in her books for all those in the room. The other gifts would be for the hostess or the one who brought people over to her house or room. I think she did this partly so that she herself would not be overwhelmed by all the love her guests showed her in return.

Corrie found many things to celebrate – a new book off the press, a letter from a friend, a special blessing she felt from the Lord, hearing the news that a person had come to know Jesus in a personal way – out would come the tea and biscuits. Or for *very* special occasions, the little fruit tarts.

As we travelled in later years, Corrie would often want to take our hosts out to dinner. They were usually reluctant to go. However, they always relented if Corrie would say she wanted to celebrate the publishing of a new book. 'A new baby is born,' she would say, 'and we should celebrate its birth.' Sometimes we celebrated the birth of a book ten times!

At the end of a party I could tell by the sound of Corrie's shoes on the staircase just how tired she was. But I also knew from the smile on her face just how happy those party times made her feel. She would often say to me later, 'Well, our time was like a foretaste of heaven.'

The most wonderful trait that I came to love in Corrie was her almost casual approach to prayer. I remember one time when she shocked a group during a prayer meeting. She said, 'Do you know what conversational prayer is?' She explained that it was 'a prayer in the heart; not a long prayer, but a short prayer, so we don't get bored!' Corrie was sometimes restless during a prayer meeting when people would pray at length and there would be a long pause before the next person would begin. She felt prayer was a time for doing business with the Lord. And sometimes with me. Corrie tried to avoid conflict with others at all times. If she felt tension in our relationship, she would tell the Lord about it in my presence. I knew about the problem then – she knew that I knew – she knew that the Lord knew – and I had no chance to explain or defend my point of view! I learned some patience and heard some important advice through Corrie ten Boom's prayers.

When someone came to her with a prayer request, she took care of it immediately. She very seldom said, 'Let's pray.' She'd just start talking to the Lord about the problem, often to the surprise and almost embarrassment of some people. If a person came to tell Corrie the sordid details of all their sins, she would stop them short. 'Repent,' she would say. 'Ask Jesus to forgive you. I don't need to hear all those things.' If a person came to Corrie with a personal problem – depression or grief or unhappiness – she wouldn't let them get very far before she would level with them. 'Do you know that I have to fight that problem too?' I could see the surprise on their faces when they heard that Corrie had personal battles in life. And then she would say, 'Now I'll pray for you, and you pray for me.' She would often encourage them with a verse of Scripture and be on her way. That was her approach to getting a person's eyes off himself and onto Jesus – and also a way not to be overcome by the problems of others.

Very often we would counsel people together. I tried to make the surroundings a little more comfortable with tea or coffee. Corrie would often have her basket of mending at her side and would hand stitch her clothes as she helped others to mend the broken parts of their lives.

It was natural for Corrie to finish a party with a prayer,

saying 'Hallelujah, Amen' in a way that everyone knew she had ended both her conversation with Jesus and the occasion. Her hands would go back to her lap and she would look at all of us as a general inspecting an army – straight in the eye. Prayer was authoritative business, and she knew her Commanding Officer personally.

The telling of stories, the talking to Jesus, the giving of gifts, enjoying parties and music – all of these traits were a part of what Corrie ten Boom called 'the joy of being at ease with Jesus'. Her faith isn't stiff or her actions stilted. She is a human being, with all human frailties and frustrations, and she knows that Jesus loves her.

11

Tramping

I went to work for 'the tramp for the Lord'. Corrie ten Boom was more accustomed to being on the go than she was to staying at home. Although I had travelled some, I am more of a stay-at-home person at heart.

I think when a person knows he has to leave a beloved place, he likes to hang onto it more than ever in his mind. I was that way with Holland. So often I longed for my own bed and the sights of my homeland – the green grass, rivers, blue skies; all the flowers and little stalls on the corners of the streets; the small shops, the market place in Haarlem with the fish cart, where men would dip and eat the herring; church bells ringing, and the carillon playing old Dutch songs. What a place to live! The *leaving* was the most difficult part. Once I arrived in a new place, I felt fine. Those years of tramping with Corrie were undoubtedly God's work in preparing me to leave Holland more permanently some day.

I had never flown before I began to work for Corrie. My first aeroplane trip was to Israel. What a thrill for me. But I think it was also a thrill for Corrie, to be able to tell me all that she knew about travelling. At such times she was very mother-ly, telling me about everything from the tickets to the seat belt.

About two weeks before that first trip, Corrie asked me to get her suitcase from the garage, so she could begin to put things into it that she thought she would need. I am a person who does things at the last minute; I prefer to stay up all night to get things ready and then sleep on the plane. But Corrie insisted that we both pack well in advance. That was always a struggle. Most of the time we took presents with us, according to the needs of the people we would meet, including little gifts for the children. The children were the ones who so often had to give up their cosy little rooms for us. Corrie's instructions to me were to always leave a present or note behind for these children. Some of the children would tell me all about the treasures in their rooms, and although they did not tell me to be careful, I could hear the concern in their voices. We always prayed that the Lord would bless these little ones for giving up their beds, and I think some of them are quite proud now that Corrie ten Boom has slept in their rooms! Most of the time she would leave a handwritten note behind.

Corrie's motto was 'travel light'. But after we packed the presents, we had to pack the props that she used to tell her stories – the torch included – then her books, and then our food. Even though meals were served on the planes, we went well prepared in case there was a shortage. We took tea, coffee, milk, bread, and biscuits. This practice stemmed in part from Corrie's concentration-camp experience and the time she spent in Vietnam, where food was scarce. We also carried a big thermos with hot water, and at times, the thermos would pop open during the change in cabin pressure. What a blessed relief when air travel became more commonplace for us and Corrie agreed to forgo the big thermos of hot water!

Finally came the clothes. Corrie was accustomed to travelling with American dresses that didn't wrinkle, but during the first trips, I often worried about how wrinkled my clothing would be. In the beginning Corrie sorted the various elements of her wardrobe and packed each set of items in a separate cloth envelope with the name of the item on the outside. Later, she replaced these cloth envelopes with wooden boxes! What a difficulty at times, to fit them into the suitcases. Travelling light often turned out to include some *very heavy* luggage.

I still have the cassette tape from our first trip. We travelled second class, as we always did. Corrie showed me where to sit and how to buckle the seat belt, and on every trip after that, she reminded me where to sit and to fasten my seat belt. I was a little afraid that first time, but the plane was soon in the air and my fears turned into 'oohs' and 'aahs'. Such freedom in flying!

I remember how overwhelmed I was with all the delicious things we were served on the plane, and I am a bit sorry that those specialities became commonplace after a while. With Corrie beside me I felt as if I had a private teacher taking me on a tour.

As the years went by, however, I took care of the travel arrangements, and it became my responsibility to make sure that the tickets were in order, the reservations made, the suit-cases delivered, and that our schedule was well planned and co-ordinated. In my role as travel agent, I learned a major lesson about how God can use our mistakes when we commit them to Him and ask His forgiveness.

Corrie told me a story about mistakes during the early days of our work that has helped me often. She once visited a weaving school in Switzerland, where she saw many students at work on the looms. She was curious about one thing, and after a little while, she asked one of the student weavers, 'Sir, what happens when you make a mistake? Do you have to take it all out and start over?'

The young man replied, 'Madam, when we make mistakes, we tell our teacher. He is a masterful artist, and he shows us a way we can use our mistake to improve the beauty of the pattern.'

That story was like fresh air to me. Instead of feeling that I had to cover up my mistakes or try to forget about them, I began to see how God might use my blunders to increase the beauty in my life.

This was to be the case on one particular trip. We had a busy week in Seattle – the weather was cold, and we had lots of snow. Corrie was in her eighties by then, and we tried to avoid severe weather, and especially snow, whenever we could. Our next stop was Minneapolis, and the weather prospects weren't much better.

During the flight to Minneapolis, I talked with a young stewardess named Beth. She was a very pretty girl with a sparkling personality. When she saw me reading The Living Bible she stopped to ask, 'Are you reading *the Bible*?' When I said *yes*, she replied, 'I've always thought the Bible was a boring book.'

I asked her if I could read her a passage, and she agreed. I read to her about the love of God – the height, breadth, and depth of His love (*see* Ephesians 3:18-19).

'Is that in the Bible?' she questioned. She could not believe her ears. I gave her a copy of *The Hiding Place* and suggested she get a copy of The Living Bible for herself. I also gave her the dates and places where Corrie would be speaking in Minneapolis.

Before we knew it, we had arrived in Minneapolis – and more snow. I looked for the people who might be picking us up, but all I saw was snow and more snow. Nobody seemed to recognize us. 'Corrie,' I said, 'maybe the snow has kept our hosts away.' I took out our schedule and went to make a phone call.

Then I discovered the mistake – we had arrived a day too early! I was shocked at my blunder and wondered how Corrie would react. She expected all of our plans to be in good order, and here we stood in a new city in the snow – without a host and a day early for our hotel reservations. I was embarrassed to tell her I had made a mistake, but there was no other choice.

Corrie was silent for only a moment and then she said, 'Well, why don't we just call the hotel and tell them we have arrived a day early? Maybe we can have a good day of rest, write a bit, and get ready for our next meeting.' Instead of being upset, Corrie took the mistake in stride and saw a possible good side to the situation.

While we were in Minneapolis, I had to leave for a couple of days to go to Rochester, Minnesota. When I got on the plane, I could not believe my eyes. Beth was the stewardess on the flight. She quickly told me that she had purchased a Bible and was reading both it and *The Hiding Place*. The flight to Rochester was short, but we had a little more time to talk, and she promised that she would attend one of Corrie's meetings.

When I returned, Corrie and I had a good time of praying together for Beth. And sure enough, she and her mother did come to hear Corrie speak. The next day Beth called and asked me if she and her mother could come to see us at our hotel. When they arrived the next day they opened a basket filled with hot tea, cookies, and cake – and spread it all out in a beautiful way. What a lovely thing to do. Only an American would think of a thing like that!

Corrie was asleep when they arrived, and while she napped, I told Beth and her mother more about Jesus. I finally asked them if they wanted to invite Jesus into their lives, and they were eager to do so. Corrie awoke just as we were praying, and what a wonderful wakening it was for her to hear a mother and daughter receiving Christ as Saviour. We had a great time of rejoicing together over tea.

Corrie and I have often reflected on that tramping incident – how God had taken my blunder and used it to improve the beauty in the pattern of Beth and her mother. If we had flown a day later, as we were scheduled to do, I would not have met Beth. Romans 8:28 took on a new meaning that day: 'And we know that all things work together for good to them that love God, to them who are called according to his purpose.' All things – even our blunders.

12

America, America

We were staying with Corrie's dear friends in Tempe, Arizona, Jack and Louise Lambert. Both are teachers, and we were left to enjoy their home and garden by ourselves each day. It was fun for me to be able to get Corrie's breakfast, especially when I discovered that the Lamberts had Gouda cheese, Dutch tea, and rusk, which are some of Corrie's favourites.

The weather was nice enough that we could enjoy our breakfast outside. The Lamberts had a telephone on the patio, and how luxurious we felt, sitting outside enjoying the early morning hours in the garden – not even having to leave to make calls or answer the phone!

One morning I answered the phone to hear a greeting from Frank Jacobson, a producer from World Wide Pictures. I had heard his name often and had read the letter in which he expressed World Wide Pictures' interest in making a film about *The Hiding Place*. Corrie had been praying about such a film for many years, and it seemed that the door was opening and the film would really happen. I had never met Frank, though, and I was startled by how fast he spoke. My English could in no way keep pace with his rapid speech! Then he asked me to spell the name of the motel where we were going to stay on our next stop. I panicked. I tried to spell the name as best I could remember it in English, but I must have confused him greatly, and when he hung up, I wasn't sure he'd call me back. Talking over the phone and meeting him face-to-face are two different things. I was so embarrassed and tense I didn't know what to do. Had I ruined all chances for Corrie's movie? He called back later that day, however, and I told him how sorry I was that I didn't speak better English. By that time he had found out the name of the motel from another person and we could laugh about the morning incident. (Later, Frank became for us 'Papa ten Boom'. Frank's beard reminded Corrie of her father. He often took care of us in a fatherly way.)

Late that afternoon I had a good talk with Jack, our host, who is an English professor at Tempe University. I told him that the panic I had felt on the phone was the same panic I felt as a child when a teacher would ask me to quote a verse from Psalms in front of my classmates. I shared with him how difficult even my own language had been for me, and that learning English was a frightening experience. Jack assured me that I was learning English the best way – trying and making mistakes as I went along, and that someday even spelling would become easy. I made a special effort after that day, however, to learn spelling, and Corrie and I would sometimes have spelling bees with our friends.

Learning English was just one of the many lessons that faced me when we came to America. America had already become like a second home to Corrie, but everything was new for me when we landed at Dulles Airport in Washington, D.C., in 1969. Right away I began to notice the people and the amount of bright colour everywhere. In those days the people in Holland wore much duller colours than the Americans – more beiges, soft greens, and grey. Here I saw reds, bright greens, yellow, and even pink in the middle of winter! Each person was like a new storybook for me. The sequins on the eyeglasses, the makeup, the lovely hairdos (even on the men), the false eyelashes, the beautiful stitching, and the heavy soles on the men's shoes. My own shoes are size $8\frac{1}{2}$, and I often felt like hiding my feet under whatever was nearest. I began to think that maybe in America I could take my feet out of hiding. People were smiling, and Corrie was explaining everything.

I had never been in such a warm, humid climate as in Washington, D.C., that day, and I was amazed at the sights and sounds and smells that surrounded me – in particular, the smell of gasoline and the sea of parked cars at the airport.

Many many more surprises were in store for me. Everyone in America seemed to be on a diet. In Holland, diets are usually for sick people – those who are diabetic or have gall-bladder problems. Being overweight is more socially acceptable in Holland, and few people go on diets to lose weight. Not everyone has to be a size 14. We spoke at camp meetings during the first trip, and I was amazed that women came to camp with round boxes – and to my surprise, they contained wigs.

The homes of our friends were dazzling to me – all so brightly coloured and decorated, especially the cheery bathrooms. I had never seen toilet tissue with flowers on it – and perfumed, no less! I knew I had to tell my mother about such richness. How our host and hostess laughed when they found me writing a letter on toilet tissue! I can recall each room of the first American home I visited – the paint on the walls, and the colours of the upholstery.

Still, the new language was the most difficult part of America to assimilate. Very often people would speak to me and I would just smile or say 'yes, no, great,' or 'I love you'. Those were the few words I knew and could say when they seemed appropriate. Much of the time the sentences came and went and I didn't understand much of what was happening.

I had my most difficulty in the South. I remember in particular one little boy who kept calling me Ma'am. He was the son of our hostess, and I felt that a boy his age should know the difference between his mother and me – you see, I thought he was calling me Mum. I became very upset with him, but finally Corrie set things straight when she explained that he was calling me Madam, and that instead of being insolent, he was really being quite polite!

Corrie would let me read aloud to her during our morning devotions, and that became one way I learned new words very quickly. We read and reread portions of Oswald Chambers'

My Utmost for His Highest every morning for nine years. We also read our German and English mail. I kept a dictionary close by, to look up new words, and I also kept a notebook so I could write down words I heard and look them up later. Mostly, though, I learned by trial and error in my associations with people. Different friends helped me in different ways.

Billie Barrows helped me to worry less about my mistakes. I had a habit of saying, 'That is a beautiful dress, isn't?' I always failed to add 'it' to the end of the sentence. When I would become upset with myself, Billie would say, 'Ellen, don't try so hard. This is you, and we all love to hear you speak with your accent and Dutch phrasing.' That was important for me to hear. If my innocent mistakes were okay with Billie, they must be okay with others. I was able to relax more. I found the Americans encouraging. We Dutch sometimes don't show as much encouragement to people trying to learn our language. Still, I worked to add 'it' to my questions.

Elizabeth 'Tibby' Sherrill, who helped Corrie write *The Hiding Place*, also helped me overcome my fear of three-syllable words. She encouraged me to shout the words that were the most difficult – and furthermore, to shout them in the shower, so I could hear myself saying them. The Dutch language does not have a *th* sound, and that was also something new for me to begin to hear myself say. Tibby's advice helped me greatly.

Slowly, and over a period of time, I began to learn the American ways and the English language – still keeping my Dutch heritage but learning to feel at home in a new culture. The many times of trial and frustration were rewarded by deeper communication, closer friendships, and new personal growth.

The stanza of one of my favourite poems says:

> Success is failure turned inside out,
> The silver tint on clouds of doubt,
> And you can never tell how close you are,
> It may be near when it seems so far,

So stick to the fight where you are the hardest hit,
It is when things seem worst that you must not
quit.

[AUTHOR UNKNOWN]

I thought of that poem often. In many ways I had to learn to be like a child again in learning a new language and feeling comfortable in a new culture. I was trying to make sense of a new world – wanting to be a part of something I didn't fully understand, relying on the help of friends to help me discover this new land.

The first chapter of James speaks about learning the *new life* of a Christian:

> Realise that they [trials and frustrations] come to test your faith and to produce in you the quality of endurance. But let the process go on until that endurance is fully developed, and you will find you have become men of mature character, men of integrity with no weak spots. And if, in the process, any of you does not know how to meet any particular problem he has only to ask God – who gives generously to all men without making them feel guilty – and he may be quite sure that the necessary wisdom will be given him.

James 1:3–5 PHILLIPS

Growing up to be like Jesus is very much like learning a new language and a new culture. Some of the customs are different, sometimes the jargon of Christianity is difficult to understand, sometimes the material trappings can dazzle us, and sometimes we need to struggle to learn just how to spell out our faith for others. We never lose our unique identities as His children, but as we grow up in Christ, we are being prepared to feel at home in His homeland someday – heaven itself.

13

Dealing With Death

The afternoon meeting was over, and Corrie was taking a little nap. I quietly entered the room we were sharing and looked over to see how she was resting. She looked very pale. I couldn't see her moving or breathing. I thought, 'Corrie has died! The Lord has taken her home.' I immediately began to think about what to do and who to call. But after a second, she took a deep breath, and I knew we were still together.

That afternoon was the first time I had confronted fully the fact that Corrie might die while I was her helper. I felt a deep concern that everything be organized, so I would know what to do in case that ever happened, and I shared this concern with Corrie. Rather than be sad at the idea, we ended up rejoicing together as we thought about all of Corrie's friends that I would be able to call upon at such a time.

As we talked, Corrie and I recalled her friend Alicia's death, and how friends had helped carry the load of grief. Corrie made many great friends in her travels, and she always warned them that they had to stay special friends, even if Corrie didn't write or see them for several years. One of those special friends was Alicia Davidson.

Alicia had inspired and motivated women around the world to become godly women and reach others for Jesus. She and her husband, Howard, had opened their home in Maryland to us many times, and on one occasion, Alicia and Howard asked

that we stay in their home while they made a trip to meet with
Christian leaders in various cities around the globe.

We two enjoyed their lovely home so much, and our friends
in Maryland spoiled us with attention and gifts, but during our
stay, word reached us that Alicia had died in Hong Kong.
Corrie felt a deep grief at the loss of her dear friend, and she
said through her tears, 'Let us read together.' We prayed and
had a time of rejoicing as we recalled the many wonderful
hours of fellowship which Corrie and Alicia had shared.

The next morning I took Corrie a cup of tea and she said,
'Ellen, I just can't believe that Alicia is no longer here, but the
Lord Jesus comforted me during the night with Ephesians
Three.' Corrie often dealt with her personal problems this way
– with taking them to Jesus in prayer and filling her mind with
the Word. She shared Paul's words in Ephesians with me:

> So please don't lose heart . . . feel honoured and encour-
> aged. When I think of the wisdom and scope of his plan I
> fall down on my knees and pray to the Father of all the
> great family of God – some of them already in heaven and
> some down here on earth – that out of his glorious, unlim-
> ited resources he will give you the mighty inner streng-
> thening of his Holy Spirit. And I pray that Christ will be
> more and more at home in your hearts . . .
>
> Ephesians 3:13–17 LB

Corrie has been comforted in part by remembering that so
many of her pleasant hours with Alicia had been times when
they were both looking for new ways to minister to others.
They had encouraged each other spiritually.

In the days that followed, Corrie and I found ourselves
ministering to Alicia's other friends and comforting them in
their grief by recalling Alicia's friendships and her devotion to
ministry. Corrie grieved for her friend, but she worked her
way through that grief by doing just what she and Alicia had
done together – sharing Jesus with others.

As Corrie and I recalled that time in our lives. I was able to
look ahead without fear to the possibility of Corrie's death. To

Christians, death can be a time for rejoicing that a loved one is with Jesus. It can be a time for encouraging others and finding a new place of ministry to friends and relatives. What a great thing to be able to face the idea of death with peace and joy. I had not been able to do that for many years.

My father had died when I was just starting my nursing career, and the scars were deep from that experience. Papa left early in the mornings, and he was usually gone by the time we got up. He came home, however, at the same time each evening on the same bus, and we children always went to the bus station to meet him. Papa was a carpenter, and I can still remember how strong his hands felt and how he would hold my hand as we walked home from the bus station together.

One day he told me that he was working on a new hospital and that he had worked on the top of the building. I was afraid of heights, and I knew that Papa had epileptic seizures. I was afraid that one day he would fall from those high beams.

When we would get home from the bus station, Papa would sit in his chair and read his newspaper. Mama served him coffee, and Papa would often fall asleep. Mother told us that he needed a little rest after a heavy day of work, and it was only much later that I recognized this habit as a symptom of *petit mal*, the form of epilepsy he had. In my younger days, I saw my father as strong and hard, yet somehow I recognized that he had an inner weakness that I couldn't quite understand. I didn't know the full depth of his depression and emotional brokenness during those years.

One day while I was working in the hospital, the director sent for me and told me when I entered her office that my father was very sick. By the tone of her voice, I knew that Papa was more than sick, and I asked her if he was still alive. She shook her head no, and then I asked her if he had taken his own life. He had.

The day of Papa's weakness had finally come. He had not fallen from a high building as I had feared as a child, but life itself had become like a high building to him, and he had become afraid to walk the beams.

God must have been preparing me for some months for that moment, because He had given me a Christian roommate in the hospital. Her name was Corrie, too. She had told me about the Lord, but I was fighting her evangelistic efforts very much. I was afraid to give up the idea that I was not a Christian by just going to church and trying to be good. I felt I was concerned about other people and I tried hard to help my patients with a laugh and uplifting word. I often sang the old church hymns I had learned as a child, to encourage my patients. That was a common practice at the hospital where I worked. Each day we nurses would begin our work by singing for the patients in the hall of the hospital, and then the director would give a short Bible message.

Sometimes when I was alone in our room, I would pick up some of my Christian roommate's books and after my father's death, those inspirational books became a source of real strength for me.

I had faced death in the hospital many times, and I had learned how to share the grief of a patient's family. But my father's death was different – he had not died from a disease – and my own personal world seemed to fall apart. The answers that I had for my patients and their families didn't seem to work for me. The room of the director, already a rather dark room, had become even darker to me that day I learned my father had taken his life. The November days in Holland are already cold and terribly windy, but that day I felt frozen from within.

I seemed to walk through a dreamland during those first few weeks after his death. I tried to be strong for my mother's sake. Some dear friends opened their home to us, for we could not go to our own home.

The last memory I had of my father was of him sitting at the table by the window, playing solitaire. As long as he was playing, we children were not allowed to talk with him. After I became a Christian, I struggled with many guilt feelings about that memory – thinking how I might have tried to break that false protection and reach my father. That last view of my father was etched deeply into my being, and for years, I found resentment brewing in me when I would see Corrie playing her favourite game of chess. I would feel hopeless, pushed out, unwanted.

My father's death brought about a real thirst for God in my life and it actually led to my total commitment of my life to Jesus in a personal way. After my conversion, I had to boldly face several facts that were important for my healing from those deep wounds.

The first fact was that there was nothing more I could do for Papa. All of the *if onlies* had no benefit. They only hurt me further. The word *if* had become a big word in my life, but it never brought me any peace, and I had to let go of it.

I also realized that I had to leave Papa in the merciful hands of Jesus. I had to face the fact that I did not and *could* not know my father's heart. We can never know what goes on in the inner life of another person. It was not up to me to judge Papa's exact relationship with Jesus.

And the third thing I learned in this time was that we must force ourselves to *remember the good* in other people. The first thing I now ask a person when I have heard their mother or father committed suicide is this: 'What is the happiest thing you remember about that loved one?' I remember the little walks with Papa from the bus to our home and how strong and secure his hand was to me.

The death of Conny, Corrie's first secretary, was much different. I have a long list of good memories about Conny. She had taught me so many lessons about life – not only lessons about how to be a good companion for Corrie. Conny had a gift of making each person that she met feel special. She had suffered as a little girl in a Japanese concentration camp, and every person and situation she encountered after that seemed like a special gift to her.

Conny and her husband were preparing for a mission to India when she became ill. During those days she had thought a great deal about packing suitcases and taking only the most necessary items along. Deep in her heart she was also busy preparing for a different trip, for Conny knew she was seriously ill.

One day Corrie and I found ourselves back in the hospital where I had once worked, this time to visit our dear sister in the Lord. Conny couldn't talk very much, but every word she said seemed like gold.

I wanted to talk about life and getting well, and when Conny asked Corrie and me to sing Psalm 23, we skipped the verse that referred to the 'valley of the shadow of death'. Conny knew that, and her only remark at the end of the song was 'one more verse'.

Conny said to Corrie later, 'Tante Corrie, this will be the first trip I will take by myself. Mother or Father went with me when I was a child. Then you were with me on all our trips, and since you, my dear husband. But this trip I need to take alone.'

Her husband was there, and he took her hand and said, 'Con, I'll take your hand and will only let go of it when Jesus is here to take hold of it.' This one sentence took the fear of death out of Conny's heart and also out of my heart. I hope that some-day I will have somebody holding my hand until just the moment when they give my hand over to Jesus.

As on all journeys, you like to say good-bye and leave a word behind. Conny did that for me. She laid her hands on my head – hands that had blessed so many people – and gave me a verse that I still carry through life: 'Be faithful in the face of death and I will give you the crown of life' (Revelation 2:10 PHILLIPS).

Conny's death gave me an opportunity to minister to Corrie, too. Conny had been like a second Betsie to Corrie. Now this sister was leaving her, too. When Corrie said to me in her grief, 'Ellen, you are the only one now in my life,' the words of Conny came back to me forcefully: 'Be faithful . . . '

The death of my father was an event that brought forth a hunger and thirst for the Lord Jesus. Conny's death brought forth a hunger to be faithful and to be ready to prepare others for the greatest journey of life. Conny had showed me how to pack the right suitcases and only take along the essential items.

With my father's death, I felt deadness inside, and the pain was great. With Conny's death, I felt eternal life, and the joy overshadowed the grief. The difference was Jesus.

He's always the difference between death and life – for everybody.

14

A Book-Table Ministry

'One, two, three, four suitcases, two boxes of books, and us. We're ready, Corrie.' The boxes were with us everywhere. The sale of books was the primary means of support for Corrie's work. It was also a big part of my job.

I learned a major lesson about books and manuscripts during the first few months of my work with Corrie. Corrie was still in the hospital, and I was on my way to see her with a friend. It was raining hard that day, and when we spotted two boys hitchhiking along the road, we picked them up. In those days in Holland it was a common and safe practice to pick up hitchhikers. These two boys were English, and as we drove along, we began to share Jesus with them. I didn't know as much English as my girl friend, but I *did* know about Corrie's concern that I never leave a conversation about the Lord without giving the other person some literature that might continue to help them. When it came time to drop off the two boys, I thought, *What can I give them?* Suddenly it dawned on me. I had received some books in the mail that very morning – they were copies of Corrie's latest book published in English. English books for English boys – it seemed to make sense. I had brought a copy along to show Corrie.

I wrote *God bless you* in the front of the book, prayed, 'God reach their hearts,' and we hurried on. I was eager to tell

Corrie my big story for the day – how I had given her English book to hungry hearts.

'Oh, Tante Corrie,' I said as I rushed into her room. 'You'll never guess what happened on the way over here. I gave one of your books away.'

'Which book, Ellen?'

'Well, this morning I opened the mail and found three copies of your book, *Plenty for Everyone*, written in English. I brought one of them for you to see, but on the way we gave a ride to some English boys, and I knew I should give them a piece of literature, so I gave them your book.' By now I began to suspect, that maybe I hadn't done the best thing. I didn't particularly like the look I saw in Corrie's eyes. True, Corrie was glad that the English boys might be blessed by her book, but she was *not* happy that she had to wait yet another day to see for herself the English version of her book. You can be very sure that I had a copy of her book with me the next day!

'Ellen, you will understand more later,' she said. 'Authors work very hard to write their books, and sometimes they have to wait a long time to see them published.' Corrie often referred to her books as her 'babies' being born.

I *did* learn to understand more about the importance of books to Corrie and to the ministry. I also began to understand how important books were for my own sense of ministry during those tramping years. Not only was I responsible for ordering enough books and making sure that they went with us – a responsibility that sometimes caused me anxious moments when I would wait until the last minute to place the order – I was also responsible for the smooth, behind-the-scenes sale of the books at Corrie's meetings. I anticipated those times after the services with great joy, as I looked forward to meeting the people and conversing and counselling them.

One of the most important lessons I learned as I manned the book table for Corrie was a lesson about prayer. Since I didn't often have an opportunity to actually stop and pray or counsel at length with a person at the book table, I often found myself saying, 'I will pray for you.' In some situations I really prayed. At other times I would realize that I had met so many new people that those who first asked me to pray had been forgotten. How guilty I felt! What could I do? I asked the Lord to help me pray for others more effectively.

About that time the Lord brought a person into my life who had a deep love for the Lord. One of the first things he taught me was to have a feeling of commitment to those for whom I promised to pray. He helped me realize what a serious thing it is to say, 'I will pray for you.' I don't say as quickly as I once did, 'Yes, I will remember you in my prayers.' But now when I say it, I say it with commitment. I put the name of the person and the purpose of my prayer on a little card. For some persons I pray daily, mostly in the morning after my quiet time. This is an exciting time for me – almost like a visit with each person. The moment I read a name, I make a mental picture of the person, and then I pray. The Lord has answered so many requests in the lives of those whom He has given me to pray for. This was a rewarding way of continuing my ministry at the book table, long after I had left town.

Another lesson I learned was to see each person at the book table as a unique, special individual.

Corrie and I lived for a time in an apartment that overlooked a beautiful lawn – it was always so green and well kept. The gardener came every week and mowed the grass very quickly and to perfection with his electric lawnmower.

One day a neighbour asked if he could care for the lawn for a while. He needed the exercise after a severe illness, and instead of using a big electric mower, he cut the grass with a hand mower. While working in our office I could hear the little machine at work. I heard it stop and start rather frequently, so I looked out to see what was happening. I saw the man mowing for a while, then lifting the mower and putting it down. Lifting, mowing, lifting – all across the lawn. He did this several times, and I wondered why. About a week later, as I was parking the car in the garage, I noticed little bunches of wild flowers in bloom on the lawn – purple, white, exquisite, tiny things.

What had the man done? He had seen those little plants growing in the lawn. Instead of just mowing over them, he had stopped, lifted the mower, and given them a chance to grow. After some weeks, tiny flowers were in bloom everywhere.

It was so easy to be like a big, powerful, electric lawnmower. It is rather easy to sell a book and never really see the person who is buying it. I had to learn to be like that man with the little flowers – giving the people at Corrie's meetings a chance to respond and share their burdens, allowing them to begin to blossom in the Lord. A person can die in his hurt if someone doesn't respond with a caring touch or willing ear.

The book table was the financial base for Corrie's ministry. But for me, it was my chance to reach people and pray for them, to give them a chance to pour out their lives and share their hurts. The boxes of books represented all of my friends in cities around the world – and the new friends still to be made. The books were our travelling companions.

15

Winning Some Souls

Corrie worked with Mother Mitchell in Japan during her early years of ministry. Both Corrie and Mother Mitchell were real 1800s-style soldiers for the Lord.

One afternoon, Mother Mitchell said to Corrie, 'Come, let us win some souls for Jesus.' That was not a very common line to Dutch Reformed ears, but Corrie went with her, into the streets of Tokyo. They gave away tracts about Jesus, and during their walk, they met a woman with a small baby on her back. Using the only Japanese words they knew, they smiled at the woman and said, 'Good morning,' even though it was 5 o'clock in the afternoon. That must have really caused the woman to take notice, because she stopped and received a tract from them. Corrie and Mother Mitchell could tell that the woman was deeply troubled, and through an interpreter, they discovered that she was on her way to take the life of her baby and herself. That afternoon she gave her life to Jesus, instead.

Corrie kept that phrase in her vocabulary, and she would sometimes ask people to go with her to win some souls. More often though, Corrie just witnessed for the Lord wherever she happened to be and to whomever was within hearing range. Talking about Jesus and her relationship with Him was as natural as breathing. Airports were one of her favourite mission fields.

Corrie used a wheelchair in airports. She really didn't need those wheels under her, but the wheelchair helped to conserve her energy for more important times. The first time Corrie yielded to the wheelchair was a difficult moment for her – but then she saw the opportunity for ministry, and when Corrie sees a potential harvest, she ceases to care about the type of vehicle that takes her to the ripened field.

In one particular airport in Alaska, we had an hour stopover between flights. We were on our way to the mainland United States, and from there to yet another country. But as usual, Corrie didn't know she was on her way to a place of ministry. She just ministered as she went along the way of life!

While the young porter was pushing Corrie through the airport, she asked him, 'Sir, you must know your way around this airport very well?'

'Yes, Madam,' he replied. 'I have worked here for several months now, and I know every hallway.'

'That's great,' said Corrie. 'By the way, do you also know the way to heaven?'

I chuckled to myself, for I was quite sure the porter was not expecting a question like that.

'Excuse me,' he said. 'What did you say?'

And Corrie spelled out 'h-e-a-v-e-n' for him.

Very often, Corrie would open a lengthy conversation about the Lord with just that series of questions. At other times, I would explain what Corrie had said and introduce her properly to the porter. That gave me an added opportunity to tell about her ministry, explain why I was working with her, and tell the porter about the Lord. We worked together as a team in reaching people in airports for Jesus!

In Atlanta the porters have come to know Corrie well, since we have been in that city many times, often for just a quick change of planes. One afternoon a porter asked Corrie to go with him to witness to the woman who worked in the airport bar. 'I've testified to her often,' he said, 'but she says I haven't had the hard life she's had. Well, you know about a hard life, Miss ten Boom, so you must go with me.' With that, they wheeled off to the bar.

I knew that Corrie didn't enjoy going into bars, because they were dark. She never enjoyed eating in restaurants that were dimly lit. She would become especially upset when we walked into dark restaurants from bright sunshine. Once I said, 'Tante Corrie, in a little while your eyes will get used to the darkness and you will see better.'

'Yes,' she answered, 'and that's a good example, Ellen, about the way sin works. If you are in the darkness of sin constantly, you get used to it. You forget what bright light is.' Still, when it came time for witnessing, Corrie would overcome even her dislike of the dark, because she knew she was bringing the Light in with her. Corrie went with the porter that afternoon, and I went to check the tickets and to pray that the Holy Spirit would prepare the heart of that woman. Corrie had to hurry to catch the plane, but we praised God together for His work in that woman's life.

Travelling as we did, we discovered that many hours can be wasted in restaurants while waiting for the food to come. We acquired a habit of using those moments to write letters or read the Bible or prepare a message.

One time in Russia, we played a little game to witness to those at neighbouring tables. I asked Corrie all about how to become a Christian and why Jesus was important. I asked questions about the Cross and about sin and salvation. Corrie explained everything in clear, simple language, and it was amazing to us how the conversation stopped at the nearby tables and the people ate in silence to overhear what we said. Then to make sure that 'I understood everything correctly,' I asked Corrie to also explain in German. Corrie repeated all she had said and closed in prayer, teaching me how I might accept Jesus as my personal Lord. What a way to witness to the Russians!

To Corrie, evangelism wasn't using a formula. She might use the same words and techniques over and over – and yet each time was new for her, because the people and places and circumstances were different. So much of what I know about evangelism I have learned from Corrie – not because she openly taught me, but because I was able to observe her offstage and in the ordinary moments of life. Corrie was always ministering – not just when she was on a platform in front of an audience. Telling others about Jesus was her life.

I, too have found special opportunities to witness during my times away from Corrie. After five years of travelling, I became ill, and a kind Christian doctor diagnosed my difficulty as exhaustion, instructing me to slow down and rest more often. 'You have sinned,' he kindly said. 'The Lord says the seventh day is for rest, and He has given you a body which He calls a temple. Ellen, you have not been resting, and you have not been taking care of your temple.' Friends had been encouraging me to learn to rest more, but I knew that rest was easier said than done, especially when one is trying to keep up with all the work that a Corrie ten Boom can generate! But Corrie also saw my need for rest and recreation, and when we were in California, she and our friends Ed and Thelma Elfstrom made arrangements for me to go to a spa.

My first reaction was that a spa was a waste of time and that I had more important things to do. I looked at the people in the spa, and most of them seemed only concerned about their weight and figures. Then I began to look at the situation through the eyes of ministry. Suddenly, I saw that some of the people at the spa might also have deeper needs and that the Lord may have planned my visits to the spa for the most important task of all: sharing His love with another person.

One evening I was sitting in the whirlpool bath after a hard workout, and a girl asked me who I was. I introduced myself and told her about my work with Corrie and about my relationship with the Lord. She said quietly, 'Yes, Ellen, I knew the Lord, too. But now I have to find *myself*. I used to teach Bible studies, but I really cannot stand Christians any more.'

She related more of her life to me, and I could sense a real need for friendship. I needed a friend, too, so I said to her, 'I'd like to be your friend, and I could use your friendship, too.' And we began to look forward to meeting each other there at the spa several evenings a week. Two years later, I received a lovely letter from this girl, telling me that she had found a new life in Jesus Christ.

In all my experiences of winning some souls for Jesus, I have come to realize that witnessing really isn't an event or an activity. It is a way of life. What sometimes seems to be a waste of time . . .

> sitting in wheelchairs, waiting in airports,
> sitting in restaurants, waiting for food,
> sitting in spas, trying to relax . . .

can so often be a prime moment for the greatest work of all: sharing Jesus. The Lord who redeems lives can also redeem time!

16

A New Friend and a New Ministry

Once again we were at an airport. Our flight had been delayed for an hour, so we had encouraged our hostess and friends to go on about their tasks for the day, assuring them that we would enjoy the time alone together for a walk around the airport and a cup of coffee. Corrie and I always felt a little sad at leaving a city and the dear people we had come to love so much in so short a time. We would often use those transition moments in airports to get ourselves ready for the next stop. Corrie had a great gift for putting a bottom line under the events of the past and looking ahead to the next opportunity for ministry. We would talk about the needs of the people at the next city and pray for them, asking the Lord to prepare our hearts and the hearts of the people we would meet.

We also took this time to look over our schedule. Tired from the busy activities of one city, we could become even more tired just by looking at the schedule for the next stop. Corrie would often say, 'Ellen, we need to try to arrange it so that I have a couple of days of rest first.' We did try, but it was usually impossible. The first day Corrie was in town, the newspaper, radio, and television reporters began to call for interviews.

Corrie had her own special way with reporters. They wanted to talk about Corrie ten Boom – her life and work. She wanted to talk about Jesus. And Corrie generally got what she wanted, much to their frustration at times. She considered even an interview an opportunity to share her faith. She closed nearly every interview with prayer. We knew that these interviews were important so that people would know Corrie was in town, but they were also tiring.

The early years of our travels were quite different. Corrie would work for several days in the same church, and I would have time to meet with groups of women and take part in Bible studies. I loved that type of schedule, because I could really get to know individual people. We had opportunities to share deeply in one another's lives, and we could laugh and cry together like family. In many ways, those days reminded me of my work at the hospitals. A nurse finds no greater joy than to wheel a patient out to the car to go home after she has seen the patient at death's door and spent days or weeks nursing him back to health. Many times I would see people in those churches who were *spiritually* at death's door, and what a joy it was to watch them become well during our stay!

After *The Hiding Place* was published, our schedule changed drastically. The auditoriums became bigger and fuller, and our stay at any one place became shorter. This was especially true after her appearance on Robert Schuller's 'Hour of Power' television programme. Dr Schuller was preaching a series of sermons on the Beatitudes, and he was seeking a special guest for the programme that dealt with 'Blessed are those who are persecuted for my name's sake.' His staff called all over the world in search of Corrie, and they finally found her in Colorado Springs – a short distance away for us tramps. We flew to Los Angeles, and that was Corrie's first appearance on American nationwide television. We noticed the increase in audience size almost immediately. People began to recognize her at airports. No longer did the news travel by word of mouth that a woman from Holland was in town with a great story to tell. Instead, the media spread the word far and wide, adding a new, important, but tiring aspect to our travels.

This trip was to be no different. The schedule before us said that the first hours were filled with appointments with church leaders and reporters. The days were tightly planned. And once again, I was flying to a city and to people that I did not know. In just a few short hours we would be transported from what had been to what would be. I shall never forget the many times I have walked from a plane to an airport hall. That was always a walk of expectation for me. We never knew for sure if the people would be waiting there to meet us, and often we did not know who they were. Sometimes our hosts only knew Corrie from a photograph. At other times, we were entertained by people that Corrie knew well. In those cases, Corrie told me as much as she could about the people before we arrived. Whenever I was with Conny, she would tell me about the families that she had met during her travels with Corrie, and I had carefully written down her descriptions of people and things to remember about Corrie's friends in different cities. This time we were headed for Detroit, and our only hope for the busy trip ahead was the fact that Corrie knew our hostess very well and I had a thorough description from Conny.

Our hostess in Detroit was Eleanor Barzler, one of the founders of Winning Women – a group that had grown from sixty to three thousand women in less than ten years. These women attempted to reach their neighbours and friends. They met together for a weekend every six months to have Bible studies and small seminars.

I recognized Eleanor the minute we got off the plane, and I felt very much at home as soon as I heard her soft-spoken voice and saw the way she greeted Corrie. Eleanor's youngest son, Jim, was with her, and he helped us with our suitcases. I learned from people like Eleanor how important it is to allow your children to become involved with your friends and the people you meet. The children may not like being asked to help with luggage at the time, but often these experiences are rewarding in later years, when they see how they have helped other people.

I could tell from the way that Eleanor and Corrie began to

talk that Detroit was not going to be a very quiet time. The entire weekend was planned with meetings.

After a cup of tea in Eleanor and Dick's cosy living room, Corrie went to bed. This was very often her custom, since we generally arrived in new cities at the end of a day. I would help Corrie unpack just the essentials – her black Phillips translation of the Bible and her notebook – and make sure that she had a glass of water and her slippers close by her bed. We would have a short prayer and Corrie would say, 'Ellen, the rest we will find tomorrow. Don't go to bed too late.' And within three minutes after I had left her bedroom, she was asleep.

I usually made my way back to the living room to sit with the family for a while and go over the programme. Eleanor and I became friends very quickly. She had daughters my age, and I think that made it easier for us to relate to each other. Her home became a relaxing haven for us, and down through the years we have been back many times – always feeling at home and loved. I felt free to do the laundry in the cellar and make breakfast for Corrie and myself. At Eleanor's house, I never felt foolish going out into their yard to pick apples and make apple sauce, or to gather evergreen boughs for a simple centrepiece. With the Barzlers I could be myself and share honestly the things that puzzled or upset me. I have many wonderful memories of times spent beside a blazing fireplace or shopping in the nearby precinct.

Eleanor was a superb hostess. She could prepare an elegant luncheon faster than any person I have ever met. Within fifteen minutes she could set the table with apples, nuts, tea, cheese, and crackers – letting the guests help themselves. I admired her special gift of being so relaxed about entertaining.

A shoe shop near Eleanor's house had a particular style of shoe I like, and Eleanor and I would make a trip to that shop every time we visited her. She once gave me a beautiful blue dress for special occasions when Corrie and I needed to dress elegantly. I felt like the Queen of Holland in that dress! (That was also the dress which I wore the first time I met my future husband.)

But more than these physical acts of kindness, Eleanor showed me the gift of encouragement. Sometimes I thought of myself as being plain and without the grace and charm of the lovely American women I met. When I confided these feelings to Eleanor, she was quick to point out how God equips each of us differently and gives to us the exact qualities that make us unique vessels for Him to use. 'You have many facets to your personality, Ellen,' she would say. And it always made me feel good for her to tell me that my Dutch ways were charming and that I had the heart of a homemaker. Even though she works very hard, Eleanor always found the time to sit down and talk at length with both Corrie and me.

After two days in Eleanor's house, she said to me, 'Ellen, why don't you speak during the weekend?'

'I?'

'Yes, Ellen, you. Many of the girls are single in our meetings, and I believe you could relate to them and help them by sharing some of the things God is teaching you about ministry and fulfilment as a single person.'

Ellen de Kroon speaking? I had never thought about it. To get up before so many people alongside other speakers who were very talented and used such eloquent words to deliver their messages? The very idea made me shake all over.

On one of our first trips to America, Corrie and I had attended a Christian women's-club luncheon. Corrie was the featured speaker, and the women asked me to give the invocation. I did not even know what the word invocation meant, and Corrie was several seats away. Finally I leaned over to whisper to her, 'What does that mean?' And she told me it was a little opening prayer. I had no idea where to begin to say a prayer in front of those women, but the Lord brought to mind several Scriptures that I had memorized in English, and I just recited those Scriptures together and closed with 'in Jesus' name, Amen'.

The women did not know that I could not speak nor understand very much English – but *I* knew!

As I became more familiar with English, I would say a few

words during Bible-study groups or women's meetings. Occasionally I would even give a short testimony or introduce an audience to the content of one of Corrie's books. But speaking to groups of people in a formal way? That was something else!

In the first place, I felt that I didn't have anything to share. I hadn't been through the sorrows that Corrie had experienced. I had not known the horrors of a Ravensbruck concentration camp! Oh, I had had my struggles, and many experiences, but I didn't think those experiences could possibly be of any interest to anyone but me.

Still, Eleanor had confronted me with a challenge, and I had to face the idea of public speaking. I talked the idea over with Corrie, and she felt that I could and should do it. I knew I had to prepare very well, and I began to study my Bible intensely. I prayed that the Lord would equip me with the words I needed. In that preparation time, the Lord showed me that He was the only source of help that I needed and that what I had to say didn't depend on *my* experiences, but rather, on His precious Word. And isn't that true for all of us – it's His Word that counts far beyond our experiences!

I accepted the challenge to speak, even though I was very afraid. When I got up before the women, I looked into their faces and the Lord seemed to say to me, 'Ellen, look. This is not a crowd; those are individual women just like you.' When I saw individual people instead of a crowd, I felt free. A new area of ministry was open to me. The words of 2 Timothy 1:7 came to my mind: ' . . . For God has not given us a spirit of fear; but of power, and of love, and of a sound mind.' As I began to love the women in that audience, the fear melted away and the words came to my mind.

The speaking challenges that have followed that first experience have been varied. One time I spoke for Corrie at a university meeting. Dr David Messenger, Corrie's personal physician in America, encouraged me here. I shared much about Corrie's life and work. One of the questions the students asked was if Corrie would have helped the Arab people if they had been the ones put into the concentration camps instead of the Jews. I answered with Corrie's own wise and gentle answer, 'If you see a child falling into deep water, would you jump in to save his life?' Many of the other questions were political in nature. I learned that day that we can often tell another person's story and say things about them that they cannot say about themselves – all for the glory of God. It was a rewarding experience to be able to use Corrie as an illustration in pointing others to Jesus.

At times, the reception was not a warm one. One of the most difficult speaking experiences can be on a Christian campus. So often the chapel sessions are required, and too often the services are poorly planned. You can tell right away that the students don't want to hear you when their feet are up on chairs and they are reading newspapers! Whenever I found myself speaking to newspapers instead of to people, I knew I had to rely even more upon the Lord and the power of His Word. So often He would supply just the illustration or Scripture that would cause the newspaper to drop. I have found that it is always best to be myself and to share my life, instead of trying to preach a sermon, and that it is *always* God's Word that touches hearts and changes lives.

One day Corrie had spoken twice and by the evening service, she was too exhausted to speak again. I was called upon to fill her place. I went to the church bubbling over, but after I had spoken, I felt empty and a feeling of heaviness came over me. I used the prayer that Corrie prays after her talks: 'Lord, cleanse away all that was of *me* with Your blood, and bless and multiply all that was of You, in Jesus' name I pray, Amen.' Still, the heaviness did not leave, and I told the Lord the next morning, 'Lord, yesterday was the last time I intend to speak. I will do everything else, but no more speaking.'

Then I left my room to take Corrie a cup of tea and to have our quiet time together. When I entered her room, I found that she was ill. She was supposed to speak in a couple of hours, so I prayed earnestly for the Lord to heal her – and to heal her quickly! After all, I had just told him that I, Ellen de Kroon, wasn't speaking any more.

So what did Corrie do? She looked at me and said, 'Ellen, please tell them I cannot come, but make yourself available.' The host and hostess arranged all the plans immediately, and I found myself in a position where I could not do anything else but go and speak. God rather forcefully showed me that He had called me beside Corrie to help her and that this morning, she needed help in this area and I was the one to do it. Time was short and the engagement was an important one. The meeting was to be the inauguration of a new president at a major college! A women's group, a small church service, a group of students in a question-and-answer session, a student chapel – fine! But in the face of my declaration *not* to speak, God put me in front of one of the most prestigious audiences I could ever have faced; professors, businessmen, community leaders, university students. And then the Lord showed me how He could work it all for good. I had a blessed time of preparing the message, and I repented for my defiance, asking the Lord to use me wherever He wanted to use me. The entire service was a joy, and the speaking went well.

I remember one word from after that meeting: *neat*. The students came over and told me that my talk was neat and that I was neat and that they loved my neat dialect. (In return, I told them how I thought it was neat that Americans could change a gymnasium so quickly into a formal auditorium!)

Later I had time to reflect on other special things – how God had supplied a wonderful friend like Eleanor, who would encourage me to explore a new avenue of ministry – how wonderful that God had supplied a series of growing experiences and opportunities to share His Word with a variety of groups – but most of all, how encouraging it is that in the areas where we are the weakest, Christ becomes the strongest. I know what Proverbs 18:10 means: 'The name of the Lord is a strong tower: the righteous runneth into it, and is safe.' I know where to run for strength when I have to speak before any group or to a reporter or television camera. He is the best platform on which to stand!

17

Hurricane Ellen

Corrie and I were visiting our wonderful friends, Mike and Fran Ewing, at their home in Florida. Their home was another of our special havens of rest during our travels. Outdoor girl that I am, I loved those visits to Florida's sun and beauty. The flowers and vines, the abundant colour, and in the background the deep blue sea and swaying palms – how I love to walk along the beach there!

The Ewings were a special inspiration to Corrie and me. Very often, we would make their home one of our first stops when we went back to America. With my background as a nurse, I was impressed with Mike's innovative designs for handicapped people. He is handicapped himself – without use of his legs and only partial use of his arms – and yet he regularly drives a car, even pulling a trailer, and takes complete care of himself. I never cease to marvel at Mike and Fran's creativity and the delight they show in sharing with others.

With Mike and Fran I learned the meaning of the American phrase 'let your hair down'. Fran was a true friend, who would openly point out to me areas in my life that needed the loving work of God. I could be very honest with her about my personal fears, and her advice helped me to relate to others and minister to them more effectively. What a wonderful thing to have a friend like that! In return, Mike and Fran confided some of their problems to us and gave us the opportunity to share our opinions and minister to them. While Mike and Fran were blunt and open with us, they hid from the public so that we could have time for rest and recreation out of the public eye. In all, Florida was a special place for us, because the Ewings were special friends to us!

During one of our visits, Hurricane Carmen also seemed to be coming for a visit. Mike made a chart, on which he drew the hurricane's progress according to the news reports, which said that the meteorologists had clocked Hurricane Carmen's winds at 170 miles per hour. The nearby air base was being quickly evacuated, and Mike had already made arrangements to have their boat pulled up on the shore behind their house. Everywhere we looked, we saw people making preparations to leave the area. We were busy, too, helping the Ewings load their house trailer and packing suitcases. Just two days before, we had unpacked it all. Occasionally we would stop to pray together. We were not afraid. As Fran calmly said once, 'Our times are in God's hands. We have the trailer and money to go inland to a motel and the wisdom to know what to do. Most importantly, we *know* we are in God's hands.'

I was amazed to see how all of nature responded to the coming storm. The air seemed heavy, and the birds were making strange noises. The Ewing's dog was very nervous. It looked as if we could wait until morning before our evacuation would be necessary, so before we went to bed, we knelt to pray and boldly asked God to alter the course of the storm so it would bypass the area and hurt neither people nor property. Some people think God doesn't pay any attention to prayers like that and that prayer can't change the course of a storm. I don't understand their reasoning. If we can believe God for *any* miracle or believe that He has control of *any* part of nature, we should be able to believe that God has control of hurricanes and can change their courses – and that He will act on our behalf when we call upon Him with faith.

Corrie and I went to bed, but even before we fell asleep, Fran came in to tell us that the news reporters had just said that

Hurricane Carmen had bypassed our area. The morning papers the next day reported the amazement of meteorologists that a hurricane of that strength had done so little harm and that not one person had been killed.

Corrie had been through earthquakes and hurricanes and other natural disasters, but this was the first time for me, as of course we don't have hurricanes in Holland. I learned a great lesson – a spiritual parallel about how we approach disasters. Isaiah 25:4 became very real to me with its reference to our Lord being a 'refuge from the storm'. David says in the Psalms that 'He maketh the storm a calm, so that the waves thereof are still' (107:29). Those days in Florida were the first time I had fully come to grips with the wonderful assurance that we are the Lord's and He is ours, whether we are blown away to Him in heaven or stay on earth to ride out the storm. Either way, we are His and He is ours.

It was also in Florida that I was forced to confront a tempest in my own soul: anger. Corrie and I were living in a small cottage on the beach, finishing the manuscript with Jamie Buckingham for her book *Tramp for the Lord*. Typing never has been my strongest skill, and it is a major effort for me to sit behind a typewriter. With the flowers in bloom outside and the surf rolling up on the beach – well, you can imagine how difficult it was for me to be enthusiastic about an afternoon of typing! To make matters worse, it was a hot day, mosquito bites were bothering me, and it seemed I had to retype passage after passage over and over before I could get them right. As the afternoon wore on, I became more and more upset and impatient, until finally I ripped the paper out of the typewriter with one giant *whoosh* of rage. When I looked at Corrie across the room, I saw great sadness in her eyes. She didn't say anything – I wish she had – but a great sense of failure overwhelmed me, and I ran out of the house and down to the beach. Even once outside, I couldn't appreciate all the beauty around me. A storm was raging: Hurricane Ellen!

As I walked along the beach, the Lord seemed to be the eye

of my hurricane. He spoke calmly to me, 'Why are you so up-set, Ellen, that you acted angrily? You only act the way you *are* inside. You have been angry inside for a long time. The sin is not the way you exploded at the typewriter. The sin is the anger that was in your heart. Now that it has spilled out, we can deal with it.'

I began to notice the waves rolling up on the beach. Each time they washed up on the shore, they took away some of the debris that was lying on the sand. As the tide moved in, it cleansed the beach. I asked the Lord to do that same work in my heart – to roll in and wash away the ugly debris cluttering up my life. 1 John 1 :9 seemed to ring in my ears: 'If we confess our sins, he is faithful and just to forgive us our sins, and to cleanse us from all unrighteousness.'

I walked back to the house, noticing how much cleaner the beach was than when I had left the house in anger. I knew my heart was cleaner, too, and that once again I could face the typewriter. Corrie was still sitting where I had left her. I asked her forgiveness, for I knew that I had hurt her with my out-burst. She forgave me, as she always did, and we prayed together.

I wish I could tell you that I was never angry again, but I can't. Yet another time while working in Florida on a book for Corrie, I became frustrated and annoyed at my limitations in being able to write and type freely. Fran was trying to help me, and this time I showed my anger to this dear friend and once again stormed from the room. I had been unable to com-municate freely, and out of that frustration came fear, and out of the fear, anger.

There in Fran's bedroom I fell to my knees. But this time I went one step beyond recognizing that my anger was a part of my sinful self and that it caused pain to others. This time I didn't see only sinful, suffering Ellen. *This* time I also saw how Jesus Himself had suffered on the Cross for my anger. He had *died* for my anger. I am not sure exactly what happened to me as I knelt there, but as I confessed and repented of my anger to the Lord, I felt a deep, deep release in my spirit. It was as if the

Lord was cutting away that part of my nature as a major act of divine surgery.

So often when I do things that I don't like, I am reminded of those storms in Florida. I am forced to recognize that what I *do* is a reflection of what I *am* inside. The confession must not only be for my errors and bad deeds, but for the sin inside that caused my actions. With that confession comes a recognition that the Lord Jesus suffered so that I could have newness inside and that my old sinful nature could pass away.

This type of confession and repentance is more than asking the Lord to break up the hurricane or send it another way. It's asking Him to keep the weather conditions of my heart from developing a storm in the first place. I like the translation of 2 Corinthians 5:21 in the Living Bible: 'For God took the sinless Christ and poured into him our sins. Then, in exchange, he poured God's goodness into us!' That's a promise to claim daily for a sunny and calm weather report in your soul!

18

Finding the Christians

Trips to communist countries were always adventures! I love challenges, and these trips were filled with them. I shall never forget the first trip to Russia. When Corrie and I arrived at the hotel, Corrie was so tired that she went to bed immediately, but not before she had suggested to me that I 'go out and find the Christians'. That was to become my mission in several places around the world.

In most of the cities we visited in Russia, I knew no one when I started out. I would walk the streets, keeping my eyes open for a church. Sometimes a bus or taxi helped take me to the few addresses I had. I learned a great lesson in the process of finding the Christians in these countries: never underestimate the value of an elderly person. Often I would find older people lovingly at work in the churches, scrubbing the floors or dusting and polishing. As I tried to communicate with them, they would lead me to someone who could speak German or English, and they in turn would introduce me to the pastor so I could ask him if Corrie could come and bring a greeting. These elderly people were the real catalysts to bringing a Gospel message into those churches. I learned that one doesn't speak or preach in Russian churches – but some *greetings* can take more than half an hour to deliver!

One night Corrie became ill and was unable to bring greetings to a church group in Moscow. I was asked to bring greet-

ings for her. I was a bit nervous about speaking, so I chose
Psalm 23 as the text for my greeting, since I knew this Scripture so well. I was one of seven speakers that night – a normal
occurrence – and it was a great experience to see how each of us
had one part of the same message. The people in that church
thoroughly enjoy what everyone has to say about the Lord.
That made it easier for me to speak, and I longed to linger after
the service and get to know the people. However, when the
service was over, the people all disappeared quickly – and I did
likewise.

Another interesting custom in the Russian church happens
while people are speaking. The congregation members write
their prayer requests on tiny bits of paper and pass them down
from the top of the balconies all the way to the front. What a
sight to see these prayer requests falling from the balcony like
snowflakes while I was speaking!

Often, Corrie's work in Russia was among the German-
speaking people. One year we went to eastern Russia, just
above Pakistan, and we had a blessed time of fellowship in the
home of a veterinarian surgeon and his wife, who was a pedia-
trician. We had a meal together, and they told us that a group
of Christian brothers and sisters was close by. They travelled
for *hours* to be with 'the woman whose books had encouraged
us so much'. I said to our hostess after the meal, 'Let us help
you clean the table.'

I knew washing dishes was no easy task, and I wanted to
help her, but she said, 'No, we will just leave everything on
the table.'

Later I understood her answer. If the police had come, we
could have honestly told them, 'We are having a *celebration*.'
I caught a new meaning of what it means to be gathered around
the Lord's Table that night.

On the way back to the hotel that night, we rode in the open
jeep of the doctor. That was the only time that his wife and I
had to share personally about some of the trials of the Christian
life in that Russian province. I sometimes wonder if I could be
strong enough to stand some of the tests given to those dear

brothers and sisters. I thought that no one would be able to overhear us that night as we bounced along the rough streets. Later, I wasn't so sure. One of our greatest fears in travelling to communist countries was that we might somehow be putting others into danger with our visits. I prayed that night for wisdom and a sensitive spirit.

The next afternoon we started for the house of our friends, taking a Christian Russian girl with us as an interpreter. We asked the taxi driver to let us out so we could walk the last few blocks to their home.

As we were walking, I felt uneasy inside, and when I glanced behind me, I spotted two men disappear into a little driveway. I felt we were being followed and told my suspicions to Corrie in Dutch. As an experienced underground worker, Corrie knew better than I how to be careful. She just continued her stroll, taking my arm, and never questioning me when I said, 'Tante Corrie, your shoe is untied. Let me tie it better.'

As I leaned down to tie Corrie's shoe, I could see two pairs of trousers disappear very quickly behind some shrubbery. From that moment on, Corrie and our Russian friend and I ended our discussion about the Lord and the friends we were going to see. Instead, we talked about the beauty of the greenery and flowers.

Finally the street dead-ended at a farm, and we sat down on a bench there and opened our Bible to pray, 'Lord, we desperately need a sign. Please let these two men come out of their hiding, so we will know whether to go to our friends' house or return to the hotel.' At that moment a dog started to bark in the next garden, and the two men showed up suddenly on the street – with no other choice than to walk back up the street. Thanks to that dog, we knew for certain that we were being followed and that it would be best to return to the hotel. A car followed us as we took the bus back to the centre of town, but we changed buses twice en route, and apparently they gave up on us and returned to the doctor's neighbourhood. Our Russian friend later told us that the two men had stayed in the doctor's neighbourhood until the next morning.

Corrie and I thanked God often for giving us special wisdom that day. It would have been so easy to put others into jeopardy. What a release it was later to hear from that family that 'all three of your cousins are doing well'. That meant that our friends had not suffered because of our visit.

Corrie and I reached the Russian people not only in their own country, but one day on a trip to Israel. Some months before our Israel trip, a friend gave me a supply of *Daily Lights*, devotional books written in Russian. I knew that one day I would have an opportunity to use those devotional booklets, so I gave them a special place in our office until the right moment revealed itself.

As I was packing our suitcase for a trip to Israel, a thought came to me again and again that I was to take those Russian booklets with me. I asked myself, *Why Russian books to Israel?* Well, through the months I had learned that I had best listen to that small voice, and those booklets got a safe little place in my suitcase. I prayed that they would arrive in the right hands.

When we landed in Israel the airport was crowded, and I noticed that there were many people coming from other countries. Suddenly in front of us a group of people appeared – they looked like Russian Jews! I followed them with my eyes and saw an airline stewardess take them upstairs. I quickly went to my suitcase, asked Corrie to wait, and ran up the stairs to where I knew I had a mission. The airline stewardess was very kind when I told her that I had some gifts for the Russian newcomers and that I was from Holland. Many of the Israelis feel kindly towards the Dutch because of people just like the ten Booms, who helped them during the war years. She opened the immigration door with her master key, and I caught a full view of my mission field.

I spotted a little woman who was crying, and I walked over to her and knelt down. My words couldn't comfort her, but I hoped my smile could. Then I showed her a little booklet from my suitcase, and when I opened it, I wish you could have seen how her face changed to surprise when she discovered that it was a book in her own language. Very quickly she spread the word to the others, and in no time I had given away all of my booklets. I thanked the stewardess and with a *Shalom* went back to Corrie. I told her about bringing the books and about giving them away. I think her heart was refreshed. She was always happy to see me doing just what she would have done had her legs been younger. Even more, I think she was happy that I had learned to be sensitive to that small voice of the Lord and to obey His command.

Corrie was so accustomed to that small voice of the Lord that she would sometimes make plans to visit a city or country even without an invitation. That was the case during our trip to Cuba. Most of the churches were closed, and we had received word that many Christians were in prison. Christian literature had been confiscated and Bibles burned. But Corrie heard a voice say, 'Go,' and we arrived in Cuba with one suitcase filled with Christian literature.

'What do you have in those suitcases?' the customs officer asked us.

'Those are books written by me, and I am going to give them to my friends,' said Corrie.

My heart was having a difficult time staying in my body. I prayed for a miracle as Corrie continued. 'Here,' she said, reaching for a book, 'let me give *you* one, and I will autograph it for you.' The man took the book and waved us through customs without further inspection.

We were met by a travel guide from Intourist, and he took us to a hotel. He kept our passports and tickets. I didn't speak Spanish, so I couldn't find my way around Havana. I only had a few phone numbers. 'Surely,' I thought, 'I can reach a Christian brother who will come and help us.' I tried calling several numbers, but got no answers! That night I became very afraid. No contacts. No passport. No tickets. Would we ever be able to leave this island?

The Lord comforted me with Acts 18:9-10, 'Then spake the Lord to Paul . . . Be not afraid, but speak, and hold not thy peace: For I am with thee, and no man shall set on thee to hurt thee: for I have much people in this city.' I looked at the city in the rain, the dark conditions for ministry, the old hotel room, and yet I could be comforted. Out there *somewhere* in the night were the Christians, and it was my challenge to find them for Corrie.

The next morning I was able to get a taxi, and I showed the driver the name of a street – the last address on our list. This was the only contact I had not called the night before. As I walked down the street, I was appalled at the conditions of the buildings and alleyways. The city looked as battered and distressed as the people who wandered slowly down the street. Finally I arrived at the exact address. I do not speak Spanish, so when the door was cautiously opened by a very tense man, I held my Bible and a copy of Corrie's book *Amazing Love*, written in Spanish. The man looked at the book, the Bible, and me, and it was if he were in a trance. I pointed to Corrie's name on the book and then pointed back to the area where the hotel was located, and suddenly his face came alive. Grabbing my arm, he pulled me into the room and said, '*Corrie. Corrie ten Boom esta aqui. Ella esta en Havana!*' (Corrie is here; she is in Havana!)

I was also in for a surprise. There in the room I found a group of men, the remnant of a group of pastors in Havana which had met that week to pray for God's help and guidance. Little did they expect a Dutch girl to come knocking at their door!

Corrie had a wonderful opportunity to minister comfort and hope to these pastors and other Christians in Havana. I had a wonderful opportunity to share and to love the people – and to give away my shoes! Each night I carried Corrie's books with me to the services, and one night I also took a pair of slippers with me. With my size 8½ shoes, I am always thinking about others' feet and how difficult it is to find shoes sometimes. I hoped that night to find some feet to fit the shoes I was wearing.

After I gave my testimony during the service, I sat down and bowed my head to thank the Lord for giving me the words and helping me to speak. As I prayed, I opened my eyes, to see two large black feet next to mine. I just knew those feet would fit the shoes I was wearing. I quietly put on my slippers and pushed my shoes over to the woman. I wanted to be very careful that she wasn't offended by my gift or that others wouldn't be jealous. I think she understood that. She calmly put the shoes on and squeezed my hands with the biggest squeeze they have ever felt.

I came to a new realization during those experiences with Corrie in foreign lands. When one goes out 'to find the Christians', one generally finds them. Because God knows where they are all the time!

19

Behind the Scenes

While *The Hiding Place* was being made into a feature-length film, God gave Corrie and me many special opportunities to work for Him behind the scenes. Much of the film was shot on location in Corrie's hometown of Haarlem in the Netherlands, so this gave us added opportunities to reach out to those in our own homeland. I felt as if I was on a new mission field to my own country. Both Corrie and I were reminded of the Lord's call to us to reach 'Jerusalem' – or our own country – first with the Gospel.

From the beginning of the film, Corrie and I prayed that the entire project would be for the Lord's glory and that the Lord would take all of the little and big problems and build them into a miracle. Many other Christians all over the world, called '*The Hiding Place* family', joined with us in that prayer.

And throughout the film Corrie prayed often. She was nearly always on the ground where the filming was taking place, and she found many people ready to listen to her talk about Jesus. The director of the film, Jim Collier, would often ask her to pray before the cameramen filmed a scene, and even the people in the cast who had never wanted to even *think* about God took off their hats when Corrie prayed. The lady with the blue coat and silver fur and black beret became a well-known figure among the camera crews.

The entire world of scriptwriting and film-making was a

new one for me. It was like a foreign country. I quickly learned, however, that even when everything seems strange, the Lord has prepared a place for us. It is only up to us to grab hold of the opportunity.

One of my first assignments was to find a group of mentally handicapped children and to help prepare them for a part in the film. Corrie always called these children 'angels'.

I had never worked with mongoloid or mentally handicapped children and had no idea how I could go about finding a group of them. I prayed for direction, and the name of a doctor's family in Haarlem came to my mind. I shared my mission with them by phone, and they told me about a school that was located opposite their house. They had seen a small bus bringing children to and from the building, and the doctor felt these might be the 'actors and actresses' I was seeking.

That same afternoon I called the director of the school. I explained the need to him and he agreed to write to the parents of the children to ask their permission. The parents all agreed, and I had my actors and actresses! I went to meet the children the next morning. That visit was the first of several as I began to learn how to work with the children and communicate with them. I loved them immediately, and from the very beginning they seemed to love me too. Some of the children were able to learn a few English words. Each day we would rehearse over and over just what was needed for the film, and soon they began to do naturally what was required: to stay together as a group as we walked through the woods and in the city, to sit together quietly while Bible stories were read to them.

I will never forget the day when our rehearsals came to an end and the children were called upon to do their part. The script called for them to be skipping until Jeannette Clift, who played Corrie in the film, called to them, 'Children'. At that word, they were to flock around her. How proud I was to see them play their part and gather around Jeannette with such loving expressions on their faces. Jeannette, too, was excited at having this opportunity to share with the children and to have a little Bible study with them. She sat with them on a bench in the park and taught them a lesson about God's love.

In another scene, along one of the canals in the centre of Haarlem, the children needed to look a little frightened. We wondered for days how we could make that happen. We really didn't want to frighten the children, who had become so trusting, and who by nature seemed to trust the universe into God's hands. But the God of the universe was also able to direct that movie scene for us. Just at the moment when the children needed to show fear, a dog broke out of the nearby crowd that was watching the filming. One of the children was very afraid of dogs, and she clung to Jeannette, just as the script asked. The director said later that he had never shot such a difficult scene so quickly and that the scene with these angels were some of the smoothest of the entire filming.

One of the most precious memories involved the wardrobe supervisor – a Jewish woman who had suffered much during the war. Clara was a very hard worker, and I still don't know how she got so many people in and out of so many clothes so quickly. I spent many hours helping her. She told me that her family members were killed in concentration camps. She had led a sad life, but she never cried a single tear as she told me her story, piece by piece.

Sometimes people can cry so much in life that they find it impossible to shed another tear.

When the film crews moved to England to finish the film, Corrie and I joined them after a couple of weeks. I again found Clara, and we picked up our friendship. I prayed that the Lord would help me to bless this friend and that the Lord would hear her heartaches. One day as Clara and I were talking, she began to cry. I could tell that she had not cried for a long time. I put my arms around her and had a prayer with her and believed that the Lord would cleanse this wound with tears and begin a deep healing.

Just two days before the filming ended, I came to say goodbye to my friend. She handed me a package. Inside was a crystal vase in the shape of a tear. This was one of the most precious gifts ever given me. Most of the time I like to make people laugh and have a good time, but this time, I had helped a person to cry, and that was even a greater blessing!

Clara was not the only person who cried during those filming days. One April morning we all assembled at 5:30 to film a scene at the marketplace in Haarlem. April is still a cold month in Holland. It seemed more like winter as we huddled in the dark in pyjamas with overcoats on. Most of the people were extras, people who, for the most part, had never acted. This was the day to film the raid of the ten Boom house. Children moved through the crowd, and the assistant director was speaking Dutch over the loud speaker, helping the group to get ready for this terrible scene. Jim, the director, had a great ability to help people feel a scene. He would talk with the actors very carefully, explaining what he hoped to see and how he thought they should feel.

On this morning he walked over to one mother who had been used quite often as an extra in the film. She was carrying a young boy in her arms, and Jim asked that she carry the little fellow a bit closer. When Jim asked her to do that, she broke down and wept. A memory of thirty years ago came alive in her mind, and she could see her own family being taken away from their house and feel herself being carried away on her mother's arm, close to her heart. That was the last memory she had of her mother, who was torn away from her and never came back. My task here was to comfort, and what a blessing it was that Corrie was sitting nearby in the Jeep, observing the scene and protected from the cold wind – again a part of that past horror. Corrie helped this woman from her Jeep.

The Hiding Place film opened many old memories in Haarlem and gave Corrie and me opportunities to comfort those who mourned with the message of Jesus' love.

As the weeks went by, our burden grew for the people who were making the film. Not just the actors and actresses, but all those who helped backstage and behind the scenes in the communities where we worked. Corrie decided to have a meeting in the concert hall of Haarlem for the cast. We found an open date and began to get ready for the meeting, asking several local pastors to help counsel. This was like coming full circle for Corrie. She had attended concerts in that hall as a young woman. During the early years of her ministry, she had held meetings in the hall for the girls' club. It was a great time we had together that evening – an opportunity for Corrie to tell her own story and to talk about Jesus to those who were in turn telling others about her life through the film. In all that was said and done during those days, God did work out the big and small problems to create His miracles – not just through the showing of the film, but through the making of it too!

While the script was being prepared for *The Hiding Place*, the World Wide Pictures team asked Corrie and me to help them create an ending for the film. As we were praying together, Revelation 3:8 came to mind: 'I have set before you an open door, which no one is able to shut' (Revised Standard Version). I shared this Scripture with the team members, and we continued to work on the script.

When we actually filmed the final scene of the film, the doors of the concentration camp swung open, so that Jeannette Clift could walk out with some of the other actors and actresses. Corrie was sitting nearby, and as she watched the doors swing open, she broke down and began to cry deeply. I knew how rare it was for Corrie to cry, and I quickly went to her side. The words in Revelation came back to my mind, and I realized in that moment why I had felt impressed with that Scripture as we planned the ending to the film. I put my arms around Corrie, cried with her, and then said, 'But Tante Corrie, God *has* given you an open door. No one has been able to shut it.' God comforted her with those words. The Lord had not only given her an open door from the concentration camp, but a door to the entire world through *The Hiding Place* film. The film would go where she could never go. That had been our prayer – and God's miracle.

20

Learning to Trust

People have asked me often, 'Ellen, in your nine years of working with Corrie, is there one lesson that stands out in particular?'

Yes. Learning to trust God. Learning what it means *to trust*. The great fear of my life was that God would let things happen to me that I couldn't handle – that He would somehow pull the rug out from under my feet.

My life seemed relatively secure before I began working with Corrie. I felt confident in my abilities as a nurse, and I knew my way around the hospital. I had my own life and friends, and I was pretty much in control of myself.

Suddenly my work changed completely. I was keeping house, cooking, receiving people who really did not need me and were not coming to see me. I was struggling to learn how to trust God for money and trying to be a good secretary. I recall taking a letter to Corrie for her corrections and approval during the first weeks of our work together. I was rather proud of that letter, but by the time Corrie finished with her red pencil, my letter looked like the worst test I had ever taken in school. Life was starting all over again at the age of twenty-seven!

Soon, however, I had traded my nice, white, stiff, secure nurse's uniform for the security of being Corrie's helper. In many ways my nurse's uniform had been my shield before the world. Now I began to feel confidence in myself as Corrie's helper, and Corrie was my new shield. I would avoid voicing my own opinion when I knew it might create a problem or an argument. Instead, I found myself saying things the way Corrie would say them. I relied on her for direction for my personal life. Corrie was my security, and I was not trusting the Lord directly for my own life. The truth of the matter was that when I found myself alone at times, I was missing a certain amount of strength. I had just traded one shield for another.

A friend shocked me when he told me that I didn't have any friends any more – that I had let myself be adopted by Corrie's friends and that although I felt secure in the role of Corrie's right and left hand, someday I would find myself alone, and I would need to discover just who Ellen de Kroon really was. I would need to trust the Lord for my own life. This friend was right, and his strong words jolted me into a search for myself and for a new trust in the Lord.

Soon after, I found myself in London with Corrie, and one afternoon I had a little time off for myself. I decided to visit a Christian bookshop that was located on the opposite side of town. Usually when I was with Corrie we would have friends drive us to the places we needed to visit – or if the place wasn't too far away, we would take a taxi. This time, however, I had to take the underground by myself. I suddenly had a fear of being locked in, and the idea of being in an underground carriage all the way across London nearly made me cancel my trip.

I repeated several Scriptures that dealt with fear, and I finally bought the ticket, boarded the underground and eventually found myself standing before the bookshop. I felt stronger by the time the day was over, but I was also deeply troubled by the experience. I hadn't been able to trust the Lord by myself for even an underground trip across London. I tried to share my feelings with Corrie, but she couldn't seem to understand my fears. I felt embarrassed, hurt and confused. That night I could not sleep very much.

The next day while I was taking care of a little Dutch baby

that had been flown in for a certain scene in the film, Jeannette Clift came and said she wanted to read some Scriptures to me. I knew I would cry, so I asked her if I could meet her later at the hotel. She agreed, and later that night, we sat together and shared some Scriptures in her hotel room. Jeannette finally said to me: 'Ellen, the Lord does not tolerate immaturity.' She encouraged me to become strong in the Lord, not relying on myself alone, but willing to trust Jesus *as my Friend*. That thought really hit me: Jesus could be my *Friend*. I had acknowledged Jesus as my Lord, but never before as my Friend. I began to see that Jesus wanted to be my personal Friend in the same way that He was Corrie's Friend. He wasn't my Friend because He was Corrie's Friend; He was just my Friend too. And a friend can be trusted! All of my longings for a personal, trustworthy friend could be fulfilled in Him.

Soon after, I was praying with a group of friends, and the Lord reminded me of a scene from my childhood. I relived that scene step-by-step in my mind. It was like a dream, only more real. I was living on the farm during the war and had been playing with some friends on the other side of the road. I must have been the last one home, because the sun was already setting. My mother came to me and told me that I had stolen something from the farm. All the clues had pointed to me, and she was very upset. Before I could defend myself and prove my innocence, she disciplined me strongly. I was angry that I had been punished for something I had not done, and I walked down to the wheat field, very upset and bitter. The wheat was drying – almost ready for the harvest. I knelt down there and prayed, 'God, I will never trust You again.' The sun had almost set by that time – but in a way, it *had* set in my heart as I prayed in my childish anger.

A scene like that from my childhood had never come back to me so vividly as it did that night, but reliving that incident also brought about a release in my spirit. I prayed, 'Lord Jesus, forgive me for that prayer, and cleanse that memory with Your precious blood.' It seemed as if the Lord opened a new door in my spiritual life that night and I could more freely and fully begin to trust my Friend, Jesus, with all my life.

Many people may acquire a trusting relationship with Jesus the minute they acknowledge Him as their Lord. But for me, trust was acquired slowly. I needed to realize my need to trust the Lord directly for my own life. I needed to see Jesus as a Friend. I needed to be cleansed from some old sins. Today I can say with much more meaning, 'My trust is in Jesus.'

21

Single

It is difficult to be a single person, whether by divorce, death of a spouse, or having never married. My greatest battle during the years I worked with Corrie was a battle against the fear that I might never marry.

Everyone seems to *know* that a woman's fulfilment is in a man and in happy children. Unless you are married, society thinks that you are only half an apple. I believed that for many years. I always wanted to marry and have a family, yet God called me alongside a fulfilled single woman and asked that I be single too, for thirty-six years. It was never my intention to work for Corrie ten Boom for nearly ten years; rather, just for a few months. But the months turned quickly into years, and the years into nearly a decade.

After I had worked with Corrie for seven years, I suddenly realized that I was in my mid-thirties and still single. That's when the uneasiness really began to hit me that I would never marry, and a feeling of loneliness overwhelmed me.

Most of the time during my travels with Corrie we shared a room. It was a real luxury to have two rooms and two bathrooms. We learned to share just about everything. But Corrie needed her rest in the evenings when she wasn't speaking, and I had work to do for her. At other times I wasn't ready for bed as early as she was, but where could I go and what could I do in a strange city with no friends?

The bathroom became a place where I could retreat to type letters or just read the Bible or a good book. Sometimes I would stop and suddenly realize where I was – sitting in a bathroom alone, in a city far from home, without any friends my age. Self-pity can really make you unhappy, and in those moments, it took over very easily. Some nights there were tears. At other times, when I was helping a hostess in her kitchen or was preparing a centrepiece for a dinner party, I would imagine what it would be like to have a home of my own and a husband and children.

It was just at this time that one of my best girl friends told me she was going to be married. I tried to show happiness for her on the outside, but inside I was depressed. I couldn't bring myself to talk about her fiancé with her, and I couldn't understand why I felt the way I did. I felt cut off from her fellowship. I wasn't jealous of her husband as much as I resented the fact that God had provided someone for her and not for me. I felt depressed even more to see them happy together after they were married. It is often easier to weep with those who are weeping than to rejoice with those who are rejoicing!

One evening I had to confess to them both that I was jealous, and the Lord cleansed my heart there and then and gave me a deep-down joy for my friend and her Christian home. I came to realize that I was not losing a friend, but gaining a new friend in her husband, and today we can write and share as we had before.

Even though I could be happy for others who were marrying, the loneliness in my own life lingered on. It seemed people were always trying to marry me off to someone. Sooner or later, almost all conversations that involved me turned in that direction. Often the questions implied, 'What's wrong with you, that you aren't married?' I knew my family in Holland sometimes wondered. My sisters were married and had children; why not Ellen? I began to wonder the same thing myself.

I was amazed that people never thought to ask Corrie about marriage. They seemed to figure that God had called her to singleness and that she was long past the age to marry. They could accept her calling to a single life, but not a calling like that for me. I was frustrated at their attitudes, yet to be quite frank, I really didn't want God to call me to be single all my life any more than they did!

Finally I had to come to grips with the issue. I knew that I could not go on being miserable and always longing for another way of life. I didn't feel that God was calling me to be single, but I knew that marriage might be months, even years away, and that in the meantime God could make me a fulfilled and happy person. I refused to remain 'half an apple', with no sense of purpose or ministry. God Himself would be the other half of my apple!

It is interesting, I think, that the Master said to a woman by a well who herself was thirsting for the love of men, 'Drink from this well . . . and you will never thirst again.' (*See* John 4:13.) He was referring to Himself. It seemed the Lord was also saying to me in those days, 'Yes, Ellen, My love is capable of satisfying the deepest human longings.' I grew to realize that only Jesus could *fully* understand my needs, and only He could meet them.

As my mind moved away from the miseries of a single life, I began to learn new lessons and see new advantages in being single. Most of all, I saw that God doesn't want single persons to be miserable before they marry; or to fail in single life and expect success in marriage; or to hurt until marriage heals them; or to waste precious time as a single person watching to catch the first glimpse of 'God's choice for my life'. He wants us to be happy, productive people, whether we are single *or* married.

Jesus was single. One evening I was at the home of Billy and Ruth Graham. Their home is so warm and simple, with flowers everywhere. I could sense the happiness of the Lord there. Billy said to me, 'Ellen, how can you be happy as a single person?' I thought about that for a moment, realizing that by the time he asked me this, many of my earlier struggles no longer existed and that I was, indeed, happy. 'Mr Graham,'

I told him, 'my need to be needed by someone else has been met by the Lord Himself. Jesus gave His entire life for others, and I feel if He could do that, I can. He promised to give us the same strength He possessed.'

Paul, too, was fulfilled in his ministry, and by his own words he found contentment in the state in which he found himself. So was Corrie. I didn't need to look very far in my search to find a single person who was fulfilled in her ministry. Corrie had more time to devote to a single-hearted search for Jesus because she was unmarried. She had more time to devote to writing books and speaking. She was free to travel and give of herself. She once said to me, 'It is best for tramps to be single.'

The secret to fulfilment is in giving. When I looked at the lives of single people who were fulfilled and happy, I also saw that these people literally gave away their lives for others. Each time I began to feel a lonely moment coming on, I looked for some way to do something for someone else.

Not too long ago, I called Corrie to see how she was.

She said, 'Oh, Ellen, I am so tired.'

Corrie was being honest with me, and she had reason to be tired. Just two weeks prior to my call she had undergone an operation to put a pacemaker in her heart, and the operation was both painful and tiring. She found herself feeling self-pity, so she put on her big black shoes, took some tracts and books, and went out to knock on her neighbours' doors. In the course of her visiting, she found a woman who was suffering with cancer, and she had an opportunity to share Jesus with her.

I thought to myself, *That's Corrie. Through her giving, her own needs were met.*

Giving provided a way of expressing myself as a woman. As I began to find ways of giving each time I felt lonely, I saw that God wanted me to be feminine and express myself as a woman. Just because I was single I didn't need to think and act more like a man. I saw that God had provided me with a very large and loving family – the Body of Christ – wherever I was. I took every opportunity that came my way to be with the children in the homes where we stayed. I cooked and sewed and cleaned house whenever the hostess would let me. I found an outlet for all those domestic chores that I love to do! And not only was I less lonely, I learned some great secrets from some great homemakers – secrets about running a household and entertaining guests.

I began to see how God had even given Corrie 'children' as a single woman. Isaiah 54:1 says, 'Sing, O barren, thou that didst not bear; break forth into singing, and cry aloud, thou that did not travail with child: for more are the children of the desolate than the children of the married wife, saith the Lord.' Corrie has never had any physical children of her own in this world, yet she has so many spiritual children that she cannot begin to count them. I wonder if there is any other woman in the world today who has had so many children named after her. We have received hundreds of letters telling us about newborn 'Corries' named in her honour. And what a joy it was to receive an announcement about the birth of a 'Corrie Ellen'. I felt so rich.

I learned this lesson in a special way during our trip to Lausanne for the Congress on World Evangelism. Corrie and I had taken a tape recorder to give to some of our Cuban brothers we hoped to meet in Switzerland. My greatest problem was in figuring out how to get in contact with them, since they did not speak English. I wandered through the Great Hall for some time, seeing many familiar faces, but none of them Cuban. I prayed that the Lord would arrange our meeting, and in just a few minutes after my prayer, I saw three of the Cuban men I was seeking. My first prayer was answered, so I prayed a second one: 'Lord, help them to understand what I am trying to do.' It was rather difficult for them to believe that I wanted to give them a nice small tape recorder, so they could take home all the tapes of the Congress. While we were trying to communicate, a young girl from America walked up to us, and I shared with her what I was trying to say. She was able to interpret for me, and all five of us ended up rejoicing together.

After my Cuban brothers walked away, the young girl began to ask me questions about Jesus. We talked about the Lord, and I shared with her how she could accept Jesus in a personal way in her life. Behind us was a large map of the world, with a counter showing the number of people on earth. The numbers changed every few seconds to indicate the new babies that were born into the world. There, under that sign, I had the precious privilege of showing a young seeker the way to Jesus and of helping to deliver a new spiritual baby into our world.

God has special ministries reserved for single people. One of the greatest lessons God taught me during my single life was that He had special ministries for me just because I was single. I was able to counsel other single people as no married person could. I began to see the reason behind some of those lonely nights spent in the bathrooms: I now had more sympathy with other people who were experiencing loneliness. My knowing that Jesus could fill the void in their lives and take care of their aches had a ring of authority to it, because I had been there!

What was even more interesting to me was that God gave me many unique opportunities to counsel and minister to *married* women. Some of these women had never really learned to trust God, so they had no idea how to begin to trust their husbands. Others felt that they had married too quickly – they felt cheated of their freedom or that they had married less than God's perfect choice for their lives out of fear that they might never marry. I had struggled with some of these same feelings. It had been difficult for me to learn to trust God and to learn to trust Corrie. I, too, had felt stifled at times. So I could sympathize with these women, who would often readily admit to me that they could never have shared their feelings with another married person. They would have been too embarrassed to admit that they had problems in their marriages.

God is the best matchmaker. Travelling as we did, I found it difficult to make friends on my own, let alone get to know men properly. I might have dinner with a man and then a few days later be thousands of miles away, with no plans to ever return to that city.

Early in my work I had got to know one special man. I met him at a church meeting where I had been invited to speak to a group of single men and women. It came as quite a surprise to me later to discover that almost all of the people in the group had been married at least once. To me, *single* had meant *never married*. I didn't know any divorced people in Holland at that time.

This particular man and I went out together several times. I had noticed some children's toys in his car one evening, but it had never dawned on me that *he* might be divorced. That news came one evening while we were having dinner in a restaurant. He told me that his wife had left him when he became a Christian and that he had three little children. As soon as he told me he was divorced and why, I felt that it was the best thing to stop right there and pray for his wife – that she would become a Christian, too, and that their home would be reunited. That was a difficult thing for me to do, but I knew that it was the *right* thing. From that moment, I felt peace about our relationship, and knew that I shouldn't go out with him any more. Still, I hurt.

As I went to sleep that night, I had a dream that affected me deeply. My dream was almost like a vision. I saw myself in a room filled with television sets, many people and machines. I saw a door, and knew that the man who walked through the door would be the man for me. Then I awoke. God seemed to speak quietly to my heart that *He* would do the arranging for that time and that I needed to trust Him for the man who would someday walk through that door. I had gone to bed quite upset, but when I awoke from that dream, I felt a wonderful sense of peace. I no longer felt any need to go out and try to find God's choice for my life. I decided to let Him arrange my life so that someday my path would cross with His intended choice for me.

As I struggled through those lessons about singleness, I saw how God was refining me and giving me a greater sense of my own identity. I acquired a stronger image of just who I was in Jesus, and I began to accept myself as an individual. Jeannette Clift, who played the part of Corrie in *The Hiding Place* movie, helped me understand a little bit more about my own ministry and talents. We read the Scriptures together often during the filming, and Jeannette one day pointed out John 15:11 to me: 'These things have I spoken unto you, that my joy might remain in you, and that your joy might be full.' And then we read together in Colossians 4:17 ' ... Take heed to the ministry which thou hast received in the Lord, that thou fulfil it.' What a blessing those Scriptures were to me! I could praise God for giving me a very special gift – the gift of being single. With that gift came new opportunities to minister, a new understanding about myself, a new understanding about Jesus, a new trust in God, and a new level of emotional and spiritual health.

I pray that my single sisters everywhere will see that God has that same gift for them, and that they will accept His gift and use it for as long as they are called to be single.

22

Prepare Me for What You Are Preparing for Me

The 1974 World Congress on Evangelism in Lausanne, Switzerland, was a high point for both Corrie and me. We met people from many different countries, some of whom Corrie had known twenty-five years ago, during the early days of her ministry. Some had been in prison for their faith in Jesus; others faced persecution when they got home. The speakers were all outstanding, with messages that blessed everyone there. We all seemed to meet at the foot of the Cross together, and people who would never have even met one another in their own countries became like brothers and sisters at Lausanne. Each day was filled from morning to late at night. Corrie had numerous interviews with radio, television and magazine reporters.

The Bible studies in the morning and the times of prayer and sharing were the most special to me. These study times only lasted for a few minutes, but looking back, they seemed like hours – so rich were they with truth from the Bible. After the formal lesson, we formed small circles and shared with our group what we had learned most from the lesson. Then we prayed together.

One morning I was late for the Bible-study time because I had been with Corrie for an interview. I had to sit in the back. When it came time for prayer and sharing, I looked around and saw a lovely American woman, with beautiful eyes. The morning's Bible study had dealt with suffering and persecution, and I thought to myself, *That woman doesn't know anything about persecution.* Suddenly I wished that I had been on time, so I could have sat at the front with brothers and sisters from underprivileged countries, where the suffering and persecution were great.

But this woman reached out and touched my shoulder and said, 'Ellen, can we pray together?'

I turned and said to her rather haughtily, 'But do you know anything about persecution? Can you help me to be prepared for suffering?'

'Maybe I can,' she said. 'Early in my life I learned a prayer: "Lord, prepare me for what You are preparing for me." I knew that I could not prepare myself for persecution and suffering, but that He could prepare me for *whatever* was ahead. Little did I know that my husband was to die on the mission field early in our marriage.'

'Who was your husband?' I asked.

'Nate Saint,' she answered. 'He was one of the five men killed by the Auca Indians in South America.'

I had thought I was sitting in the wrong place that morning, but the Lord had put me in exactly the right spot. Her prayer became the major prayer of all my tramping days with Corrie: 'Lord, prepare me for that which You have planned for me.'

In October 1975, when I found myself on a plane to Tulsa, Oklahoma, I prayed again: 'Lord, prepare me for what You have prepared for me in this city.'

Corrie and I had been invited to speak in Tulsa by the Tulsa Christian Fellowship. While we were there we also had to speak at Oral Roberts University. As the plane circled above Tulsa, I added, 'Lord, use us this week to minister peace in this city; may we be used to bring Christians together. Lord, use this week for lonely people.' I had no idea just how wonderfully the Lord was to answer my prayer.

During our time in Tulsa we stayed with Gail and Virginia Runnels, and on one of the first nights they held a prayer meeting and communion service for us and various Tulsa ministers in their lovely home. Corrie gave a brief message on the Second Coming of the Lord, then we had a time of sharing.

During the conversation, I received a telephone call from Cliff and Billie Barrows. I had just written them a letter, telling them that I was happier than I had been for a long time and that I felt I had turned a corner in my thinking about being single and alone. I had a pleasant chat with them. Billie said, 'Ellen, how can we pray that God will give you the right husband?'

I answered quickly, 'The same way you prayed for Betty and Bonnie, your daughters. God knows the best for my life.'

As I walked away from the phone I was met by a handsome man with a charming smile. 'Hi,' he said matter of factly. 'I'm Bob Stamps, the chaplain at Oral Roberts University. I've heard a lot about you. We are really looking forward to you and Corrie being on our campus.'

Let's see – Bob Stamps. My mind did an instant replay. Someone had teasingly said to me, 'And, hey, Ellen, he's single.' Quickly I thought, *So you're Bob Stamps. Fine, but I'm not going to get involved with you. There's too much work to do here.* Aloud I said, 'Hello, I'm Ellen, and it's fine to meet you. Let's join the others for a cup of tea.' That was the beginning of our friendship.

Corrie and I were to speak on Sunday evening, and we were very busy until that night. Bob called several times during the days preceding the meeting, to discuss the service. When we arrived at Christ's Chapel at Oral Roberts University, we were amazed to find it so full. Since Corrie had reached a point where she tired more easily, I was accustomed to sitting behind her on the platform, in case she needed me quickly. Bob had introduced us to the audience, so Bob and I were sitting together on the platform while Corrie spoke. Many people

have told us since then that they were praying throughout the
service that the Lord would somehow bring the two of us together. And He surely has!

It seems rather funny, looking back, that most of my speaking during that week at Oral Roberts University was on the
single life. One evening the Dean of Women asked me to
speak to a group of women who were resident advisers in the
dormitories at Oral Roberts University. Bob was the only man
at the meeting. During the talk, he told me he was thinking:
That girl is giving her single talk for the last time. He could feel
his heart beating a little faster that night, even though it was to
take him several months to fall completely in love. He wrote on
his list of prayer requests: 'Ellen is a flower for the Lord. The
Lord does not crush flowers, but He gives them water. He
replants them sometimes, or uses them in beautiful ways to
bless and help other people. I must pray for Ellen that she will
go on flowering in this garden, or until the Lord gives her
another place.'

When Bob showed me those words later that evening, *my*
heart began to beat a little faster, too! When I got home that
night, Corrie was already in bed. The telephone rang, and to
my happy surprise it was Bob. We talked for nearly two hours.
It was a deep and meaningful conversation. My room was
right next to Corrie's, and she could hear what was happening.
That didn't bother me. We were so close we shared just about
everything. When I hung up, I heard her call my name.

'Yes, Tante Corrie,' I replied.

'Ellen, something *good* is going to happen to you!' I could
hear the smile in her voice as she used that familiar Oral
Roberts and ORU saying. I quickly went in to tell her about
my evening. I think Corrie enjoyed taking the motherly role
that night as she listened to her excited 'daughter' ask her for
permission to go with Bob Stamps the next evening.

I was accustomed to asking Corrie's consent on invitations,
since she was concerned about me and I did not want to add to
her concerns or go against any plans she may have made. I'm
just glad she gave me permission to go out with Bob Stamps!

When Bob arrived the next evening the three of us had a chance to talk for a little while. Corrie found Bob a delightful conversationalist, and before we left, she stopped us, had us kneel down before her chair, gently laid her hands on our heads, and prayed a prayer that shocked us both. She prayed, 'Lord, thank You for not taking my daughter away, but for giving me a son.'

I know I must have turned many shades of red, for I blush very easily. I began to pray silently, *Lord, can you open the floor so I can disappear?* I was afraid of what Bob must be thinking!

As for Corrie's reasons, she says, 'I don't like nonsense. I expect that when a man asks a woman to go with him, there is something to it, especially at Bob and Ellen's age. After all, they weren't children.' Typically Corrie!

When we drove away from the house, I wasn't even sure what a date was all about, so I asked Bob about his plans for our evening. With a chuckle he said, 'Well, after Corrie's prayer of blessing, I've decided to change my plans. I had better introduce you to my work a little more fully.' This was my evening off – my first date in years – and I was on my way to be introduced to Bob's work? What kind of date was that? I had heard many girls talk about their dates, but none of them sounded like this one. Did I have to speak again? That would be the fourth time that day! By now I have learned that Bob loves to surprise people, and that's what he did that night.

After about a half hour's drive, we arrived at a huge pink building, a hospital, and Bob told me that we were going to visit one of the professors who was ill. After we prayed and gave him a word of encouragement, we left the room, and Bob said he wanted to show me his favourite place in the hospital. We walked through many doors and down long halls, and finally we walked into a lovely little chapel area. I had a sense of awe and adoration in that room. Neither Bob nor I spoke. It was a tender moment for us, and it seemed we were on holy ground. Bob had spent many hours in this little chapel praying that he would be a better servant for the Master Jesus Christ. I felt privileged to be in this place with him.

Bob broke the silence by saying, 'Ellen, I want us to dedicate each other to Jesus. Everything seems to be going pretty fast. After what Corrie prayed, I think I had better give you back to Jesus and let Him show us what we should do.' We knelt together and both of us gave ourselves completely to the Lord. Bob prayed for me, and I prayed for him. The former nurse and the campus chaplain were somehow very much at home in a chapel in a hospital.

On our way out of the hospital Bob said, 'I hope we don't meet any students here. Otherwise, we'll be the talk of the campus. That's something I'd like to avoid.' As he was finishing his last word, he gulped and said, 'But there they are.' Two students passed us nonchalantly, but we heard their giggles. 'There we go!' Bob said.

Bob decided to take me to an elegant restaurant – a place he knew that students would probably not be able to afford. As we talked over dinner, we discussed many things – travel, our work, friends, family, my goals in life. We knew this first date would also be our last date in quite a while. I was leaving town the next day.

At the close of the evening Bob said, 'If I ever marry and have a son, I want to name him Peter John.' How surprised I was! My own father was named Petrus Johannes – or Peter John! God seemed to confirm to me in that moment that Bob would be the man for me.

As was true for so many cities, Corrie and I did leave Tulsa. But this time something was different. A part of Tulsa came with me, and a part of me stayed in Tulsa. Bob and I began to correspond and talk often on the telephone. Occasionally we would be able to meet briefly during our travels. I was able to visit his family in Texas, and he came to Holland to meet my family. Our love for each other grew, and soon Bob was telling me to start making preparations for our wedding. I found myself praying yet again, 'Lord, prepare me for what you are preparing for me.'

23

Wedding Doubts

During the first few weeks of my romance with Bob, I didn't realize what was happening to my relationship with Corrie. Somehow Corrie had recognized long before I had that a change was coming. She told me later that the Lord had told her during a prayer time that He was taking me away. Corrie had wondered if I might die. What a release it was for her to see what God meant. I have often thought how many people have left Corrie – people she loved and with whom she shared her life on a deep level. Corrie knew better than I that to prolong our pulling away from each other would be a painful experience. Early in the spring, Corrie and I began to pray for a new helper in her ministry.

Corrie also knew that my loyalty and love for her was deep and that she would need to push me out of the nest before I would be totally willing to fly away with Bob. The problem was that Corrie was nudging me out of her nest before Bob was ready to pull me into *his* nest! I had new lessons in trust to learn during those interim months.

I was certain that Bob was the man for me. That certainty had come one morning while Corrie and I were on the ORU campus. We were sitting in the control rooms of the television studios watching some tapes. Around me were monitors and the equipment of a television editing room. Suddenly I seemed transported to the very scene that had been in my dream a few years before. The details of that room were somehow very familiar to me. Then the door opened, and in walked a smiling, cheerful Bob Stamps. The puzzle pieces seemed to fit together in my mind, and I had a deep assurance that God was whispering over my shoulder, 'See, Ellen, how well I can organize things?'

'Yes, Lord, I see!'

I didn't try to explain this to Bob until after we were married – mainly because I couldn't explain this working of God to myself. So I didn't try to *explain* – I just *knew*!

Bob, too, had felt a divine ordering of our romance, but he also held many doubts about marriage. We discussed these fears openly during our phone conversations and our visits together. Bob knew how much Corrie valued my loyalty and how much I was devoted to her. He wanted to be very sure that marriage was God's calling for us before he pulled me away from Corrie. Bob also had a fear that he wouldn't have enough time for both marriage and his ministry at ORU. As a single man he had been able to devote himself to the students and his work wholeheartedly, and he wondered how marriage and a possible family might take him away from that ministry.

For nearly fifteen years Bob had been deeply involved in service to the Lord – as a student in seminary and then as a chaplain. He had given himself to Jesus and to His work twenty-four hours a day. He had counselled many students who came to ORU from broken families, and he could see how deeply these students had been hurt by divorce and dissension in the home. I think it is fair to say that Bob felt that if he married *anyone*, he was going to marry Ellen de Kroon. He just wasn't sure if he was ever going to marry!

During the summer preceding our marriage, Bob led a group of students on a six-week study tour to Israel. After that he went to Poland for three more weeks of soul-searching with a good friend who is also in the ministry. Corrie – and even my own mother – were in America during this time, and I was truly *alone* in Holland.

One night, with both parts of my world so far away, I had a

good talk with the Lord. I poured out to Him all the things I could still do with my life as a single woman. I even said, 'God, if Bob decides that he wants to remain single as a minister, then these are the things I am prepared to do for You if it is Your will.' Deep down inside, I knew that the Lord had closed the door on my work with Corrie. I had been taken out of that relationship, and yet some of my feelings were still tied to that work.

Do you know that feeling? You may have been a leader in a group or a part of a company, and even though your term of office or employment has expired, you continue to worry about the job and wonder how things are going? You begin to wonder if you did everything you could have done and how things might have been, if only you had made different choices? Well, I went through the *if only's* that night about my work with Corrie. 'God, if only I'd done this - if only I'd done that.' I asked the hard questions: Had I loved Corrie enough? Had I been too pushy? Had I managed my work well?

I poured out these feelings to the Lord, and as I prayed, I felt the burdens of my heart begin to lift from Corrie's work. I saw how I had continued to carry a burden that the Lord had already taken from my shoulders and placed on someone else's shoulders. That night I was able to straighten up and stand tall, free of the load, and to look at the future with boldness. I felt ready to shoulder a *new* load. If that load was to be a part of Bob's ministry, so be it. But if that load was to be a ministry apart from Bob, I knew that I must accept even that with a willing joy. I was reminded of Isaiah 61:1:

> . . . the Lord has anointed me
> To bring good tidings to the afflicted;
> He has sent me to bind up the brokenhearted,
> To proclaim liberty to the captives . . .
> [NEW AMERICAN STANDARD BIBLE]

That night I also began to sense a part of God's use of those months prior to our wedding. God was helping me to let go of the past and entrust my future to Him. But even more, He was teaching me that my trust must *always* be in Him. I had been willing to entrust my life to Bob. That seemed fun and fairly easy. I had to relearn that, far beyond my commitment to Bob, I must be willing to entrust my life to the Lord.

As I shared these lessons with Bob later – and let him know that my trust was in the Lord no matter what Bob finally decided – I think Bob felt a new freedom in our relationship. He began to see how his time would not be divided, but rather, his load of ministry would be lightened, because there would be two of us to carry the load.

Through the fears, doubts and uncertainty of those months, God seemed to be weaving our lives together in a mysterious but beautiful way. Looking back I can see how God not only brought us together, He *tied* us together.

24

Wedding Joys

I do not want you to think that all of our engagement was clouded by fear and uncertainty. Many times I felt as if I were in a hurdle race. Learning lessons about trust and commitment were times when I was crossing hurdles. But most of the time I had a sense of joy at the prospect of winning the race and crossing the finishing line! God blessed us in many special ways during our engagement – even to providing the miracle of my wedding dress.

I had never worried about personal money while I worked for Corrie. She took care of our living and travel expenses. In addition she gave me a little pocket money that I could use for personal needs. I never gave much thought to making investments or trying to save. I was working with Corrie because that was God's call on my life, not for money or for the expenses of the future. Quite by surprise I found myself facing a fact: weddings and changing countries cost money; more money than either my mother or I had.

It was May 1976, and I was in Tulsa; Bob had just proposed, when suddenly my financial burden began to weigh me down. Matthew 6:33 had been a verse I had often claimed with Corrie in times of need. Now I would believe it for myself – if I seek the Kingdom of God first, then all secondary things will be provided – and they were.

Just before I left for Holland for the final time prior to my wedding, my dear friend Thelma Elfstrom called from California to say, 'Ellen, I have just sent you money for your wedding dress. I wish I could be there to help you choose it, but I know you'll find the right dress.' What a wonderful miracle! The Elfstroms had promised me a wedding dress just shortly after I met Bob, but their gift came just at the moment of my concern. It was a *very* generous amount of money but I had no idea of the cost of wedding dresses – particularly for the kind of gown I had in mind.

I had prayed for a white wedding dress trimmed in Irish lace. I had a mental picture of exactly what I wanted. Now I had the money to go out and find that dress. You can imagine how excited I was! Jean Ann Tinsley, Bob's secretary, agreed to go shopping with me, and we set out in search of my special dress. Looking back, I realize I probably went to the most expensive shops in my quest.

We went to several shops, and my enthusiasm began to wilt. I wanted a *white* dress and I was continually faced with off-white, cream-coloured, light beige, 'candlelight' dresses. I wondered if anyone in America made *white* dresses. Then I looked at the price tags. I had never looked at wedding dresses in my life, and I had no idea how expensive they could be. Every dress seemed to be more than I was willing to spend. I said quietly to the Lord, 'This is very interesting, Lord. What am I going to do now?'

At just the moment of that prayer, a young woman in the shop came to me and asked, 'Have you been to the shop across the street?' We hadn't, so we made our way there. I told the saleslady what I had in mind – white trimmed in Irish lace – and I gave her my size. She showed me several dresses, but none of them was what I had in my mind's eye. Finally I said, 'Don't you just have one dress somewhere . . . '

She said, 'Well, I have a dress . . . ' Quickly I asked, 'What size?'

She said, 'I'm not going to show you the size before you put it on.' She came back with the dress draped over her arm and helped me put it on before she allowed me to look in the mirror. When I turned around to see myself, I discovered I was wearing *my* wedding dress! Exactly the dress I had imagined, and sparkling white at that!

'Look at the price,' Jean Ann said.

And I looked to see the exact amount my friend Thelma had sent!

'Now look at the size.'

I couldn't believe my eyes. The size was two sizes below what I had requested. Now *that* was a miracle in itself!

I asked Bob's secretary, 'Can this be real?'

She replied, 'It's the dress God wants you to wear, Ellen.'

And I knew it, too. Jean Ann and I praised the Lord there in that small dressing room. When the saleslady came back, we told her about our miracle and how she had been a part of it.

That was just the first of many special gifts which God gave us through our wonderful friends, especially those in Europe. Bob and I would have to cross the ocean soon, moving this Dutch girl and all her belongings permanently to America. Riska Bosshardt, my dear friend from Haarlem, knew we couldn't be loaded down with household wedding gifts on our journey, so she got the word around to family and friends to give money instead of pots and pans and the like – and they surely did! We were overwhelmed with the love expressed to us. Now we would have a good start towards buying the necessities for our flat in Tulsa.

During my early travels with Corrie I had met two women in California who told me, during a trip by car from Los Angeles to Bakersfield, that when I married, they wanted to give the reception. I hardly knew these women, and I hadn't really thought they were serious, although they had told me that the Lord had strongly impressed them that they would one day hostess my wedding reception. What a wonderful surprise when they and their husbands came to Holland to take part in the wedding and then for them, along with a group of friends, to sponsor and host our wedding reception at ORU!

My sisters and sister-in-law helped me sew the dresses for my three nieces who were to be bridesmaids. Many friends in

Holland whom I had not seen for almost ten years suddenly came back into my life, to surround me with love and help. One special friend was Hanna Geesink. My mother was in America visiting my sister Susan during much of my engagement – a trip she had planned long before I met Bob. Hanna helped me as my mother would have during those days.

One of Bob's desires was to be married on a Sunday, so our church wedding service was held on the 1st August, a Sunday. As is required by Dutch law, we had a civil ceremony at the Town Hall several days before the actual wedding, and also a civil ceremony at the U.S. Consulate in Rotterdam, where I promised to be loyal as the wife of a U.S. citizen, even though I retained my Dutch citizenship. As a part of this ceremony I had to sign my new name: Ellen Stamps. The fact that I was getting married and leaving Holland really hit me in that moment, and tears rolled over my cheeks. My name – de Kroon – or 'the Crown', was being traded in for an American name!

In all, I went through *three* wedding ceremonies in Holland!

I didn't sleep at all the night before my wedding. I was too excited. Instead I went over all the details of the following day in my mind. I left little notes for the Master of Ceremonies, Ben Hoekendijk, and some others. We had a houseful of family and friends, and I gave them all instructions about just what to do and when. After organizing plans for Corrie all those years, I didn't want my own wedding day to be disorganized. This time I learned that a person can even overorganize.

When morning came I opened the curtains to see a dismal sight: fog and lightning – a full-blown thunderstorm. For the last time I knelt down as Ellen de Kroon, with Hanna and Riska after they spoiled me with breakfast in bed. I prayed, 'Lord, You know we really need better weather today.' Then I quickly began to prepare for the hours ahead. Riska helped me in so many ways. Hanna had decorated the staircase with a garland of flowers – Corrie's house looked like a beautiful garden!

We were all surprised to discover that one of my nieces had

grown so much during just a few short weeks. Quickly I let down the hem of the dress, with my sewing machine plopped in the middle of the floor. What a hurried but special time.

Then Bob came to the door of the house for me, as is the Dutch custom, to bring me my bouquet which he had chosen himself, and take me to the church. We had a quiet time of communion with the minister and Bob's close friend, John Collier, before we left the house. And then we were off to the little church in a long procession of cars, all beautifully decorated with fresh flowers. A neighbour drove our car, and as we sped along, out came the sun in brilliant splendour! The day had turned out to be a bright and beautiful one, and the sun filled the little Dutch Reformed Church of Bloemdaal. (Bloemdaal means 'Valley of Flowers' in Dutch, and that is the name we have given our home in Tulsa.)

God had done a special work in Bob's heart on the morning of our wedding. He had spent time in prayer with John and had given himself to the Lord in a new way, in order more fully to give himself to me. We followed our family and friends into the church that afternoon, truly prepared to be married with our whole being.

As we walked into the candle-lit church we saw so many of our friends – from America, Norway, Germany and Holland. It was an international celebration! I was especially surprised to see the entire Jansen family – the farmers with whom I had stayed during the war. The organ played Bach Chorale Prelude 'Blessed Jesus, See Us Here' as we took our places in the seats of honour at the front of the church.

We asked that the Gospel message be a part of our ceremony, because we wanted our friends to see that Christ was the central factor in our lives. Sidney Wilson, the man who had led me to the Lord during the youth retreat in Austria, was present to give the sermon. Bob gave a blessing to our Dutch friends and promised never to take his Dutch bride away from their hearts.

After the wedding ceremony we made our way to an old inn for an outdoor reception. Actually it was more like a festival.

The bridesmaids, my nieces, performed little skits and sang songs about our lives before the wedding.

Throughout the day I had missed Corrie in a special way. I wished for her at many moments, but I knew she was busy with the Lord's work in America. What a surprise it was to hear her voice during the reception, coming to us over the loudspeaker. Corrie had sent a tape of her greetings to us:

Dear Ellen and Robert, bride and bridegroom:

I am Corrie ten Boom, speaking to you from America the day you marry in Holland. God bless your marriage.

You are beginning your walk with the Lord Jesus together. Both of you have already been living for Him for a long time, but now, hand in hand, you have both been a blessing to many, and you will be a far greater blessing as you go together. Sometimes you will not understand the way of the Lord.

Peter van Woerden gave me a good illustration. Once he held a camp for two hundred children, and he made them stand in such a way that they formed the name *Jesus*. The children, however, were unaware of what they were forming. Then Peter went onto the roof of a nearby building and took a photograph of the children. But first, he had to say to them, 'You move a little to the right, you to the left, you come forward a little.' The children asked why they had to stand for such a long time in the hot sunshine and why in that way. He told them, 'Tomorrow you will understand. I will not tell you now.' Then he had the photograph developed, and the children saw that together they had formed the name of Jesus.

We are called to form the image of Jesus. Galatians 4:19, 'Christ be formed in you.' Together with the Body of Christ you form the name of Jesus. Sometimes God will tell you to go a step backward, aside, forward. Don't ask why. Soon you will see it. What you have to do is just what Jude said in verse 21 in his letter: 'Remain in the boundaries where God's love can reach and bless you, then His name will be glorified.'

I know both of you. I know how God used you before. I know that together you will be a team and do work about which the angels will rejoice. How the Lord will work through you! Without Jesus you cannot do anything. With Him you can do everything.

Thank you, Ellen, for all you have been and done for me in the almost nine years of your life. How much and many blessings we have experienced in this important part of our life, going as joint tramps over the world.

Thank you, Bob, for the love you have given me already in the short time we have known each other. We remain fellow-warriors. You two, in the important place where you have been called to work. I go on as a tramp, but all three of us are connected over the waters through our prayers and love. We all three seek first the Kingdom of God and His righteousness; therefore all other things will be added to us. Jesus was Victor; Jesus is Victor; and Jesus will be Victor. Hallelujah! *Amen.*

After the festive reception had ended, Bob and I had a time of prayer with our families and close friends, and then we made our way to an old castle. We took with us a picnic basket and the cards, telegrams, and letters from dozens of our friends around the world. We set a table for ourselves, read the Word, read our messages of good cheer, and praised God together for giving us a new life ahead.

God had truly given us many wonderful gifts to surround our wedding – the gifts that friends had showered upon us with love, the gift of love for each other, and best of all, He had given us His love and His presence. I couldn't help but think: *If God could so beautifully bring about my marriage to Bob Stamps, just think what a wonderful celebration He must have planned for His Church and the heavenly Bridegroom!*

25

Good-bye, Tante Corrie

The day had come to say good-bye to Holland and to set sail for a new life in America. As Bob and I stood on the dock waiting for the ship and to embark on the seven-day trip across the Atlantic, my thoughts wandered back a few months to another good-bye. That good-bye had taken place at the Amsterdam airport.

It had been nine years from that afternoon in Soestdijk, when I journeyed by bus to my first meeting with Corrie and she had boldly said, 'I am so happy that God is going to give you to me.' Now the Lord had called me to a new chapter of His plan for my life. Corrie knew, too, that this was God's best for both of us and that the time for our parting had come. Still, that knowledge didn't make it any easier for either of us to say our good-bye.

The airport seemed exceptionally crowded that day. Corrie and her new companion, Pam, were en route to America via Switzerland. Pamela Rosewell is an English girl, who had worked eight years with Brother Andrew as his personal secretary. Now she had become Corrie's and my answer to prayer. It would be Corrie's first trip in nine years without me. I had been in and out of the Amsterdam airport many, many times with Corrie, and it was a familiar place. I knew, too, what was going to happen next. Whenever friends took us to an airport, Corrie would gather everyone around her and say, 'Come, children, let us pray.' This time was no different. We formed a circle around Corrie, the crowd swirling around us, indifferent to our little group with heads bent in prayer around an elderly woman in a wheelchair. I was standing close to Corrie, but she seemed far away. Already I was experiencing the pain that comes with separation from loved ones. My thoughts focused on Jesus' words in Hebrews 13:5: '... I will never leave thee nor forsake thee.' I had heard this verse many times, and I believed it in my head. That day I needed to believe it in a new way – in my heart.

Finally it was time for Corrie and Pam to board the plane. My hands automatically went to the handles of the wheelchair. I had pushed Corrie in wheelchairs through airports all over the world, and it took a conscious act of my will to take my hands away. That moment was my final release from Corrie's service. Her new secretary was taking over, and I was the one staying behind.

Perhaps you are holding on to something from the past that does not belong in the present. You may be thinking that the past was so much better, and that life shouldn't change. I know from that moment in the Amsterdam airport that when we loosen our grip on the past and let it go – let someone else take over the wheelchair – God gives us freedom and courage to face the future. God knows what He is doing in our lives, but we must first release ourselves completely into His hands.

Corrie hadn't made anything really special out of our parting, though I sensed it was as painful for her as it was for me. When I got home from the airport, the telephone was ringing. A stewardess was calling from the airport with a message for Miss de Kroon from Miss ten Boom: 'Look on the desk, Ellen, for a little note.'

I ran to the desk. I hadn't realized just how eager I had been for some final word from Corrie. I tore open the envelope and read:

My dear, dear Ellen,
    Thank you for everything you have done and for who

you have been during these important years of my life.

Continue to keep Jesus on the throne of your heart; then you will stay in the boundaries where God's love can reach you.

If you have time, go and look behind the painting of the 'Castle of Brederode'. I have written something on the other side of the painting.

God bless you and Bob very specially.

Your thankful TANTE CORRIE

7th April 1976

The 'Castle of Brederode' painting portrays a scene just outside Haarlem, and is by the Dutch painter A. Miolée. The painting is an heirloom from the ten Boom family, and on the back of the painting, Corrie had written:

To Ellen de Kroon from Tante Corrie:

As a little remembrance of the blessed years that we wandered together as fellow tramps for the Lord in many countries. It is great to know that whatever we do in love for the Lord is never lost and never wasted.

1 Corinthians 15:58 [The same Scripture which Corrie gave to me on the first day we met.]

CORRIE TEN BOOM

April 1976

That painting now hangs in our home, and each time I look at it, my thoughts wander to the days when I was tramping with the Tramp for the Lord around the world. I could say that day, as I can say today, 'Thank You, Lord, that You gave Tante Corrie to *me*.' And, yes, Corrie, it *is* great to know that whatever we do in love for the Lord is *never* lost and *never* wasted.

Epilogue

Peter John was born on the 18th May – the same date that Corrie's mother and father were both born. Some might say that was coincidental, but we would rather believe it was in God's special timing.

Often as I travelled with Corrie, I would stay after the meetings to sell the books, tapes and records we brought with us. It was a good opportunity for me to spot lonely, needy people who were looking for a word of encouragement and love. On one occasion, it was a young mother who came to me to say, 'Ellen, if I just didn't have two children, I would have time to be a missionary like you.' She didn't know how much I would have enjoyed trading places with her! But it was the Father who gave me the wisdom at those moments, and I said to her, 'Just imagine if Corrie's mother had said that. We would never have had a Corrie ten Boom. It was Corrie's mother who led Corrie to Jesus when she was just five years old. Isn't it great that God may use you possibly to raise one of these little ones to become a spokesman for God?' That woman left that evening as a very *special* missionary.

The 18th May will always be a date in our family to remember great parents like the ten Booms and our call as parents to be missionaries to our children.

Shortly after Peter John was born we sent this letter to all of his parents' friends:

1st June 1977

Dear Friends of Mum and Dad,

I was born on the 18th of May, 1977, in Tulsa, Oklahoma. Mum is doing well, and Dad is fine too, already learning how to take care of Mum and me.

I want to thank you for your prayers. It wasn't so easy getting out of Mum's 'cosy place'. My eyes were closed when I entered that bright, new, large place, and I felt two 'big things' around my head. My little heart nearly didn't get through it all, but the doctor gave me oxygen, which helped Mum as well as me. Dad couldn't believe his eyes, but he stayed with Mum and me until the very end, or should we say 'the very beginning'.

It was a pretty rough way to start, I guess, but they tell me I'm named after a Big Fisherman from Galilee who also had a 'rough start'. And he turned out great, so you can bet I will too!

Mum and Dad had prayed nine months for a little boy, and there I was! Dr Cohen, our doctor, is a Jewish man, and the moment I was in his hands Dad prayed a Hebrew prayer, that was followed by an 'Amen' by Dr Cohen.

While the doctor still had some work to do on my 'coming out place' under my Mum's tummy, I was put in a nice, warm towel, and after Dad had me in his arms awhile, the nurse brought me to Mum to get my first drink. To tell you the truth, I didn't feel much like supper about that time, or perhaps it was breakfast. It was one o'clock in the morning! And after all, I came out pretty well fed, at nine pounds, six ounces.

Last week Mum brought me home, and now I'm in my very own nursery. The teddy bear Dad had bought for me was waiting with a sign around his neck, 'Welcome, Baby'. Later in life I'm sure Teddy and I will become the best of friends. Things look very Dutch around me, or so I'm told, and everything is bright and sunny. At night-time we all have a little prayer together and we pray for all of you. Thank you for being so nice to Mum and Dad. I am looking forward to meeting all of you, and then I'll give you a little Peter John kiss. Bye for now, and thanks again for loving all three of us. I love you, and so do Mum and Dad.

PETER JOHN STAMPS